THE TOTAL BEGINNING GUITARIST

RICHARD HINMAN

AMANDA MONACO

Alfred, the leader in educational music publishing,

and the National Guitar Workshop,

one of America's finest guitar schools, have joined

forces to bring you the best, most progressive

educational tools possible. We hope you will enjoy

this book and encourage you to look for

other fine products from Alfred and the

National Guitar Workshop.

National Guitar Workshop Method
Approved Curriculum

Alfred

Alfred Music Publishing Co., Inc.
P.O. Box 10003
Van Nuys, CA 91410-0003
alfred.com

ISBN-10: 0-7390-9067-4 (Book & CD)
ISBN-13: 978-0-7390-9067-1 (Book & CD)

This book was acquired, edited, and produced
by Workshop Arts, Inc., the publishing arm of
the National Guitar Workshop.
Nathaniel Gunod, acquisitions, managing editor
Burgess Speed, acquisitions, senior editor
Timothy Phelps, interior design and photography
Joe Bouchard and Ante Gelo, music typesetters
CD recorded at Axis Sound, New York, NY

Cover photograph © iStockphoto.com / Digital Savant LLC
Guitar on cover courtesy of Fender Musical Instruments

CW01468227

Contents

About the Authors

Rich Hinman lives in New York City. He graduated from Yale University in 2001 and has since performed locally and nationally in numerous rock, pop, blues, and country bands. He currently plays in a rock band (Black Lab Project), an acoustic pop band (Crescent and Frost), and as a sideman for various singer-songwriters. Rich has a busy private teaching schedule and has taught at the National Guitar Workshop since 1996.

Acknowledgements

Thanks to Nat Gunod, David Smolover, Paula Abate, and everyone at the National Guitar Workshop; Pippa, Vadim, and Fran at the Great Neck Music Center; David Hamburger and Adam Levy for their help and encouragement; Tracy Walton and Adam Issadore for playing on the accompanying CD; and Sonia Lin for everything.

Dedication

To my parents, David and Lois Hinman, and my grandmother, Estelle Hinman.

PHOTO BY TIMOTHY PHELPS

Amanda Monaco divides her time between her jazz quartet, Amanda Monaco 4, and her all-girl "new generation cabaret" quartet, The Lascivious Biddies. She taught at the National Guitar Workshop from 1994 to 2002. Amanda plays Brian Moore Guitars and uses D'Addario Strings. She currently resides in New York City, where she teaches many students of all levels.

Acknowledgements

Many thanks to my family, Shmegley, Nat Gunod, the Smolovers, Noah Baerman, Michael Jefry Stevens, Karen Hogg, Michael Bates, Ben Cliness, the Biddies (Lee, D and Sassy), and my quartet (Jason, Fraser, and Jeff).

Dedication

This book is dedicated to my first guitar teacher, George Raccio, who shared his love of jazz with me and taught me how to "keep it simple."

PHOTO BY TIMOTHY PHELPS

Introduction

Welcome to *The Total Beginning Guitarist*. The cool thing about this book, and what sets it apart from other methods, is that it uses different styles—mostly rock, blues, and jazz—to teach you the basics of guitar. There is a lot of crossover between these three genres, and knowing something about all of them will make you a better, more well-rounded musician.

You don't need any prior knowledge of music or the guitar to begin using this book. The first 14 pages will get you started with essential information on technique, tuning, and buying a guitar. From there, you'll learn simple chords, strumming patterns, songs, power chords, riffs, scales, standard music notation, basic soloing, barre chords, and much more.

Later in the book, you'll learn about music theory, and there is even a handy chord encyclopedia with chords organized in a practical, useful way for the beginning guitarist.

Following are a couple of tips to make the process of working with this method more rewarding:

1. This book is meant to be tackled sequentially. Start at the beginning and make your way through slowly, taking time to absorb every example.

2. You'll learn faster if you make playing the guitar a regular part of your life. That doesn't mean practicing for hours a day; the important thing is that you play a little every day. This will keep you engaged and will keep new material fresh in your mind.

Throughout the book, you will see tabs on the outer portion of the pages indicating "Rock," "Blues," or "Jazz." This tells you that either a particular example, a section, or a whole chapter is devoted to one of these genres. If there is no indication, then the information is more of a general nature and applies to all three musical styles.

Now, it's time to start the rewarding experience of learning the guitar and playing great music.

Enjoy.

Track 1   A compact disc is available with this book. Using the disc will help make learning more enjoyable and the information more meaningful. Listening to the CD will help you correctly interpret the rhythms and feel of each example. The symbol to the left appears next to each example that is performed on the CD. The track number inside each symbol corresponds directly to the example you want to hear. Track 1 will help you tune to this CD.

Buying a Guitar

Buying your first guitar does not have to be intimidating. You just need to know what to look for. Here are a few pointers to help make your first purchase a little easier.

1. **Choose between an electric and an acoustic guitar.**

   Electric and acoustic guitars are played in exactly the same way. It is a common misconception that it is best to start learning on an acoustic guitar. Make your purchase based on the style of music and the sound you like. If you're a rocker, chances are you will want to play an electric guitar—likewise if you are inspired by the electric blues of Stevie Ray Vaughan and B. B. King, or the jazz stylings of Wes Montgomery and John McLaughlin. If you are into the acoustic side of rock (exemplified by players like Dave Matthews), acoustic blues (Robert Johnson), or certain types of Latin jazz (Antônio Carlos Jobim), you will most likely want an acoustic guitar.

   If you decide to buy an acoustic guitar, you can choose between one of two basic types: classical or steel-string. The classical guitar has nylon strings, which give it a mellow sound appropriate for classical or soft music. Steel strings are slightly more uncomfortable to play at first, but give the guitar a louder, brighter sound appropriate for more popular styles of music. If you are under nine or ten years of age, a ¾ size classical guitar is a wise choice.

   If you decide to buy an electric guitar, you have a huge variety of brands, sizes, and shapes to choose from. Again, if you are not yet full-grown, it is a good idea to look for a smaller guitar.

   Regardless of how you choose, all the music in this book can be played on either an electric or acoustic guitar.

2. **Have someone demonstrate guitars for you.**

   When you're at the music store, have a salesperson, friend, or teacher demonstrate different instruments for you. The sound of guitars varies greatly, depending on the wood, body shape, size, and a host of other factors. Listen to several different guitars to get an idea of what you like.

3. **Consider the size of the guitar.**

   Comfort and playability are almost as important as sound. If an instrument is too big, it'll be difficult to play, and you'll get frustrated. Guitars come in many different sizes. Electric guitars vary widely in body and neck size; for instance, a traditional jazz guitar will have a much bigger body than a guitar traditionally used for rock. Steel-string acoustics range from jumbo to standard (also known as *dreadnought*) to smaller sizes. Nylon-string guitars come in full, ¾, and ½ sizes. Spend some time holding a variety of guitars until you find the one that "fits."

4. **Buy a used guitar with caution.**

   There are some great used guitars out there, but they are riskier to buy than new ones. Have someone you trust look over a used guitar before you consider purchasing it; you'll avoid spending money on repairs later.

5. **Look for something inexpensive.**

   You do not need to spend a lot of money to get a decent instrument. Good-sounding, comfortable, inexpensive guitars are more widely available than ever. Use your ears and take your time.

Parts of the Guitar

Acoustic

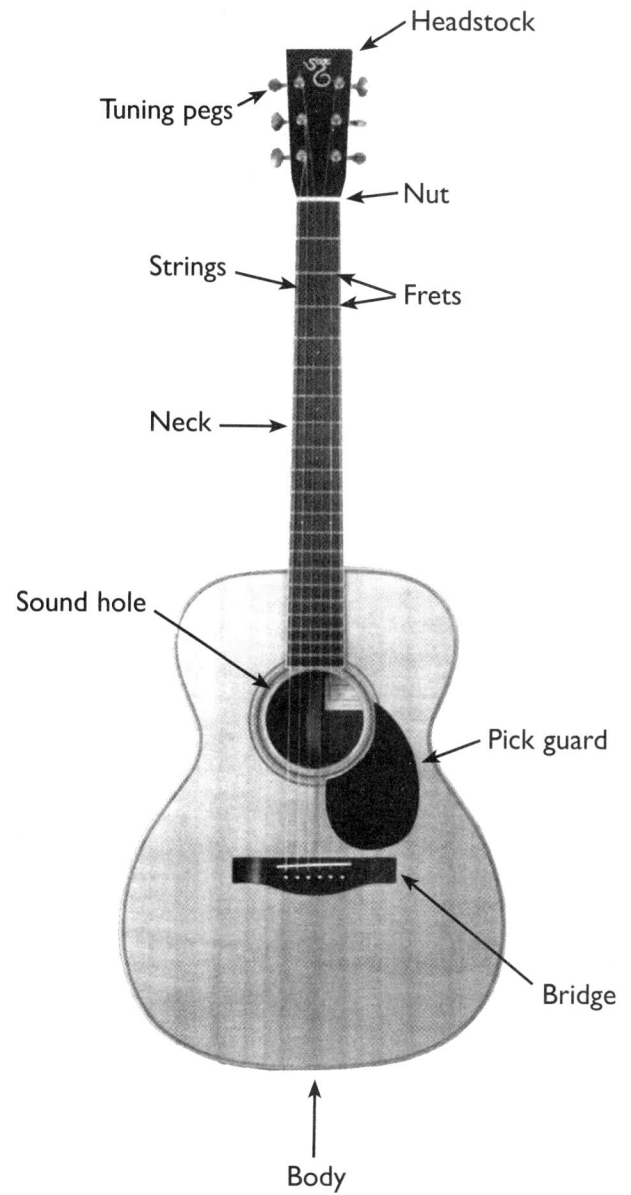

Headstock

Tuning pegs

Nut

Strings

Frets

Neck

Sound hole

Pick guard

Bridge

Body

Electric

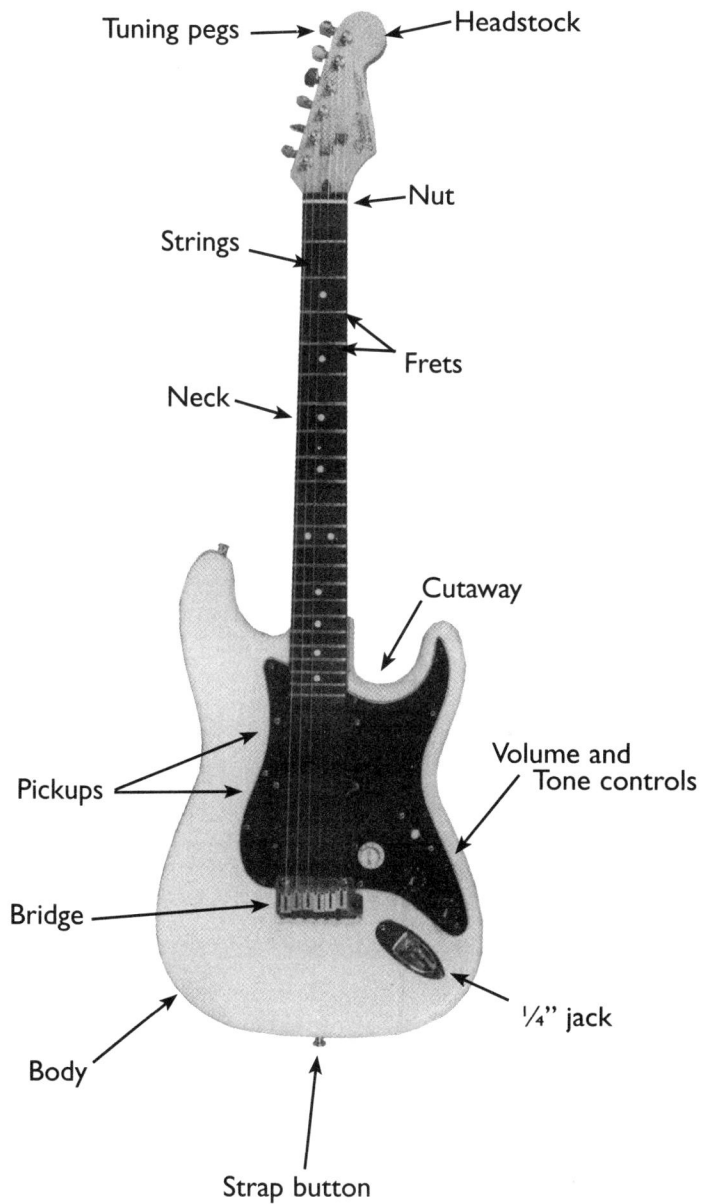

Tuning pegs

Headstock

Nut

Strings

Frets

Neck

Cutaway

Pickups

Volume and Tone controls

Bridge

Body

¼" jack

Strap button

Holding the Guitar

You can hold the guitar while standing or sitting. The following tips work for both positions. The basic idea is to be comfortable, so if you feel some strain while holding the guitar, adjust it until it feels better.

1. Stand or sit straight, but not rigidly so. You want to be relaxed, but not so relaxed that you're stooping over the guitar—it's harder to play that way.

2. Keep the neck of the guitar tilted upward. This will provide easier access to the *fretboard* (the front of the neck, where the frets are). To maintain this angle, wear a strap when you play the guitar, even when sitting.

3. Make sure that the front of the guitar (where the sound hole is on an acoustic, and where the pickups are on an electric) points straight in front of you, rather than toward the ceiling or floor.

Two Positions for Playing the Guitar

1. **Seated with a guitar strap, guitar on right leg.** The strap will keep the neck in an upward position.

2. Standing with a strap.

The strap holds the guitar in the proper playing position and allows you to move around freely.

Left-Hand Technique

The left and right hands have specific functions when playing the guitar. The left hand holds, or presses, the strings against the *frets* (metal strips that run across the fretboard). This determines the *pitch*—the highness or lowness—of the tone, or tones, that the right hand will pick or strum.

The fingers on the left hand are numbered "1" through "4." The thumb is rarely used to hold down the strings, so the index finger is given the number "1."

The frets are numbered as well. The 1st fret is the one closest to the *nut*, which is the piece of bone or plastic right next to the *headstock*. The fret numbers increase as you go toward the *bridge* (see page 7, Parts of the Guitar).

Following are some tips to help you develop good left-hand technique. Refer back to them throughout this book.

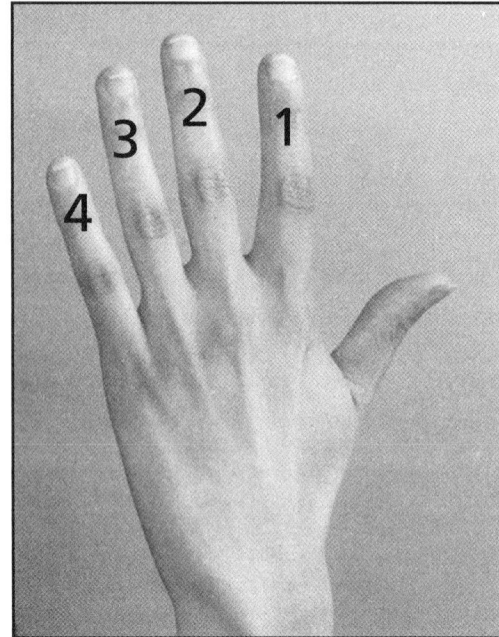

The fingers of the left hand are numbered.

1. Keep your thumb behind the neck, applying pressure against the back of the neck while your fingers press down on the strings. Do not let it hook over the fretboard or you'll have a hard time with tip 2.

2. Curve your fingers so that you are pressing down on the strings with your fingertips. This will prevent the flat parts of your fingers from holding down any unwanted notes or from blocking strings that should ring out.

3. Keep your palm relaxed and away from the neck.

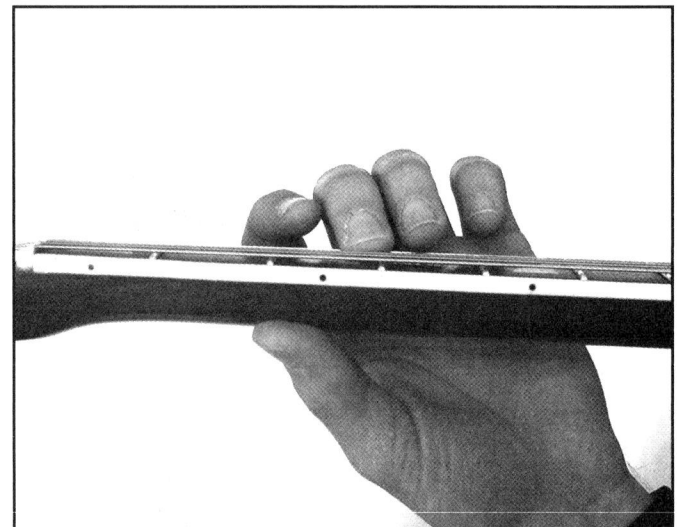

4. Place your fingers behind (just to the left of) the fret—not directly over it.

Right-Hand Technique

The job of the right hand is to strum, pluck, or pick the strings of the guitar, creating the sound and *rhythm*. Rhythm is the organization of music in time—the arrangement of long and short sounds and silences.

You can use a *pick*, also known as a *flat pick*, or your thumb alone. It can be more difficult to play with a pick at first, but once you get used to it, you'll have greater control and accuracy. Try both ways and decide which is better for you.

If you decide to use a pick, hold it firmly between your index finger and thumb, with the tip pointing away from your palm and toward the strings you are striking.

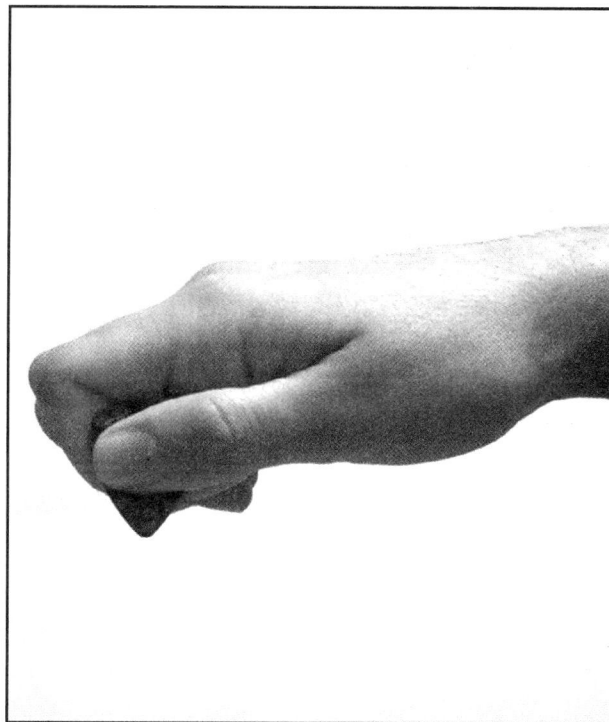

How to hold a pick.

This symbol indicates a *downstroke*, which means to strum or pick downwards, toward the floor.

This symbol indicates an *upstroke*, which means to strum or pick upwards, toward the ceiling.

A Note About Picks

Picks come in many different thicknesses. The three basic sizes are thin, medium, and heavy, all of which sound and feel different. They are inexpensive, so buy all three and decide which you like best.

Tuning the Guitar

You should check to make sure your guitar is in tune every time you pick it up to play. If it's out of tune, you can play beautifully and it still won't sound good.

Tuning is a learned skill—it may take some time to develop your ear to the point where you can do it quickly. You may break a few strings. Be patient. Strings are inexpensive and easy to change. To learn how to change your strings, check out *I Just Bought My First Guitar* (National Guitar Workshop/Alfred #22705).

String Names and Numbers

Let's start by learning the names and numbers of the strings. The 1st string, the skinniest and closest to the floor, is the high-E string (high in *pitch*; see the note at the bottom of this page). Then comes the 2nd string, B, the 3rd, G, the 4th, D, the 5th, A, and the 6th, low E. This diagram should be helpful:

Strings

	E 6th	A 5th	D 4th	G 3rd	B 2nd	E 1st
Frets						
1st						
2nd						
3rd						
4th						
5th						

Note

When guitar players talk about "high" and "low," they're referring to pitch, the highness or lowness of a musical tone. The high-E string may be closer to the ground than any of the other strings, but it has the highest pitch, so it's called "high E."

Methods of Tuning

The Piano

The six strings of the guitar can be tuned to the six piano keys shown below. If the pitch of a string is lower than the corresponding key, find the *tuning peg* (see page 7, Parts of the Guitar) that it's attached to and raise the pitch by tightening it. If the pitch of a string is higher, lower it by loosening the appropriate tuning peg. If you're having trouble hearing whether a tone is lower or higher, loosen the string until it's definitely lower than the piano key, then tighten it until it matches.

Middle C

C D E F G A B C D E F G A B C D E

1st
2nd
3rd
4th
5th
6th

Pitch Pipe

A *pitch pipe* has six pipes that correspond to the six strings of the guitar. When you blow on a pipe, it sounds the correct pitch for the corresponding string. Tune to that pitch by adjusting the tuning pegs as explained for the piano method (above).

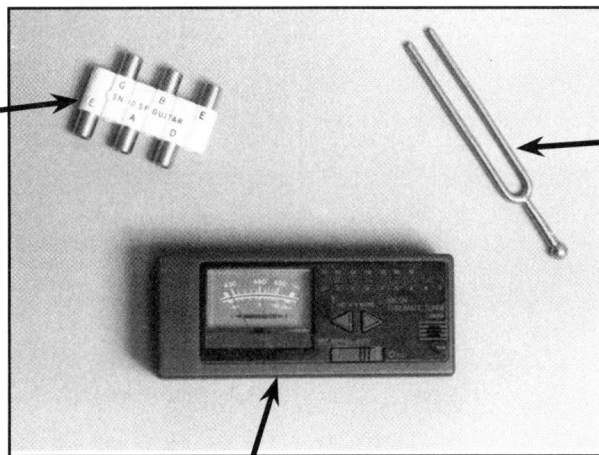

The Tuning Fork

Strike a *tuning fork* and it will sound a reference pitch of either an E or an A. From this tone, you can tune the rest of your guitar using the method of *relative tuning* as explained on the next page.

Electronic Tuners

An *electronic tuner* will "read" the pitch of each open string, telling you if it's too high, too low, or in tune. This is probably the easiest way for beginners to tune the guitar.

Relative Tuning

This is the most common method of tuning the guitar. Relative tuning takes a little more patience than just plugging into a tuner, but it has some advantages: You can tune the guitar to itself without the need for a piano, tuning fork, or tuner. It also helps to develop your musical "ear," which will ultimately make you a better guitar player and musician. Here's how to do it:

1. Tune the 6th string to the E 12 white keys below middle C on the piano. If you have no piano, use a tuning fork, someone else's guitar, or take your best guess.

2. Press the 5th fret of the 6th string with one of your left-hand fingers. Tune the open 5th string to this pitch.

3. Press the 5th fret of the 5th string. Tune the open 4th string to this pitch.

4. Press the 5th fret of the 4th string. Tune the open 3rd string to this pitch.

5. Press the 4th fret of the 3rd string. Tune the open 2nd string to this pitch.

6. Press the 5th fret of the 2nd string. Tune the open 1st string to this pitch.

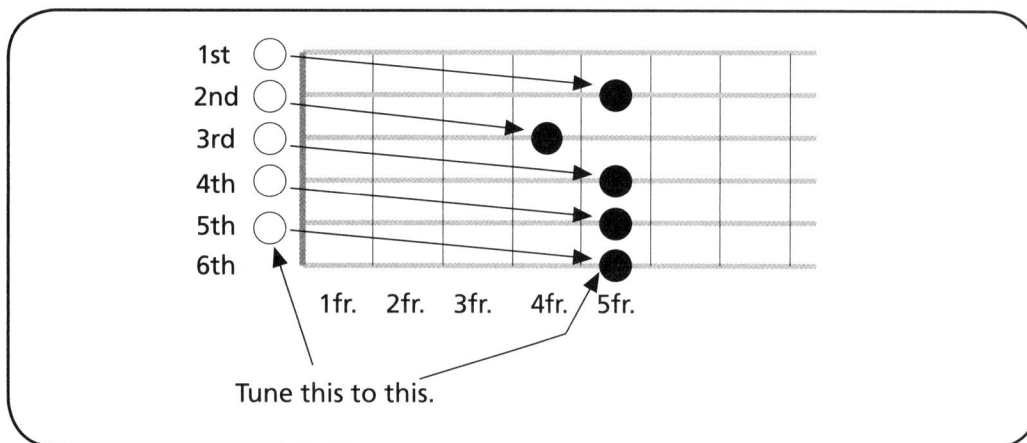

Tune this to this.

Track 1 You can also tune your guitar to the tuning notes on the first track of the CD that comes with this book.

First Chords and First Songs

A *chord* is three or more tones played at the same time. *Chord diagrams* show you how to play chords. They represent the guitar neck oriented vertically. The vertical lines are the strings and the horizontal lines are the frets. The string to the far left is the thickest, lowest string—the 6th, low-E string. The black dots show you where to put your fingers, and the numbers on top indicate which left-hand fingers to use. An "X" means that a string should not be played, and a "0" denotes an open string.

Chord Diagram

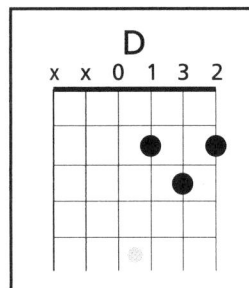

Chord name → G
Open string
Strings not played
3rd finger on the 3rd fret, 1st string
6th string
1st string

The G Chord

Put your 3rd finger on the 3rd fret of the 1st string. Strum the highest four strings by striking them downward (toward the floor) in one smooth motion with your pick or thumb.

The D Chord

Put your 1st finger on the 2nd fret of the 3rd string. Put your 3rd finger on the 3rd fret of the 2nd string. Put your 2nd finger on the 2nd fret of the 1st string. Strum down over the highest four strings.

Note About Practicing Chords

Play each new chord string by string. If a string sounds muffled, try to correct it using the Left-Hand Technique tips on page 10.

Time Signatures, Measures, and Beats

The first song you are going to play is in $\frac{4}{4}$; this is the *time signature*. A time signature consists of two numbers, one above the other, and appears at the beginning of every piece of music. The top number indicates that each *measure*, or grouping of notes, gets four *beats* (a beat is an equal division of time, like a heartbeat). The bottom number tells us what type of note gets one beat. If the bottom number is a "4," that means the quarter note (or *quarter strum*, see below) gets one beat. Every measure (or *bar*) with four beats is divided by a *bar line*. For now, we will use a single straight line as a time line for our music, and this symbol ⌠ to indicate a *quarter* (one-beat) *strum*.

The following song is in the style of "Yellow Submarine" by The Beatles. With your pick or right-hand thumb, strum down from the 4th to the 1st string, four times for each measure, counting "1, 2, 3, 4." Tap your foot down as you count each number. Try to keep the duration of each beat the same.

◼ = Strum down, toward the floor.

Track 2 In Shallow Water

Count: 1 2 3 4 | 1 2 3 4 | 1 2 3 4 | 1 2 3 4

1 2 3 4 | 1 2 3 4 | 1 2 3 4 | 1 2 3 4

* When there is no chord symbol, continue playing the chord from the previous measure.

Practice Tips

1. Break the chord change into steps. When changing from G to D, move your 3rd finger from the 1st string to the 2nd string, then put your 1st and 2nd fingers down.

2. Spend some time switching back and forth between the two chords.

3. Try the song again.

To play our first blues tune, we'll need two new chords.

The G7 Chord

Put your 1st finger on the 1st fret of the 1st string. Strum the highest four strings by striking them downward (toward the floor) in one smooth motion with your pick or thumb.

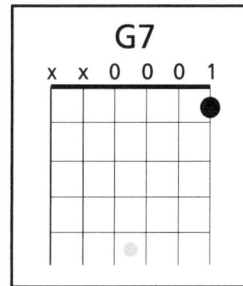

The D7 Chord

Put your 3rd finger on the 2nd fret of the 1st string. Put your 1st finger on the 1st fret of the 2nd string. Put your 2nd finger on the 2nd fret of the 3rd string. Strum down over the highest four strings.

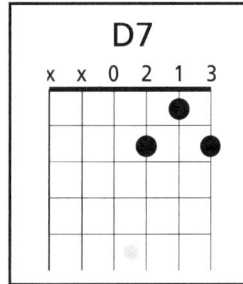

B L U E S

With your pick or right-hand thumb, strum down from the 4th to the 1st string, four times for each measure, counting "1, 2, 3, 4." Tap your foot down as you count each number. Try to keep the duration of each beat the same.

Track 3 *The Big Switch*

Practice Tips

1. Break the chord change into steps. When changing from G7 to D7, move your 1st finger from the 1st string to the 2nd string, then put your 2nd and 3rd fingers down.

2. Spend some time switching back and forth between the two chords.

3. Try the song again.

For our first jazz tune, we need to learn another new chord: D Minor (Dmin).

The D Minor Chord

The 1st finger plays the 1st string, 1st fret.
The 3rd finger plays the 2nd string, 3rd fret.
The 2nd finger plays the 3rd string, 2nd fret.
Strum down over the highest four strings.

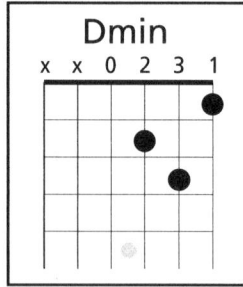

With your right-hand thumb, or with your pick, strum down from the 4th to the 1st string, four times for each measure, counting "1–2–3–4." Try to play all beats evenly and with the same duration.

Track 4 *Freddie's Bounce*

G7   etc.

Dmin

Count: 1   2   3   4   1   2   3   4   etc.

Dmin   G7   Dmin   G7

This is the symbol for a repeat sign, which instructs you to play the entire progression a second time.

Tip for Playing Chords

When changing from G7 to Dmin, do not move your 1st finger; rather, leave it in place on the 1st fret.

The C Chord and a New Rock Song

There's a new chord to learn for the next song.

The C Chord

Put your 1st finger on the 1st fret of the 2nd string. Put your 2nd finger on the 2nd fret of the 4th string. Strum down over the highest four strings.

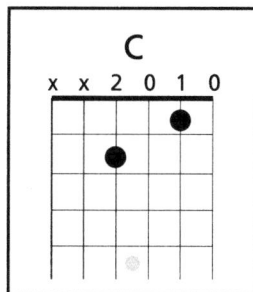

C
x x 2 0 1 0

R
O
C
K

The song below consists of the chords G, C, and D. Strum down four times each measure. For a crisp sound, try flicking your wrist a little with each strum. Tap your foot to keep a steady beat.

Track 5 *Three-in-One*

G   C etc.   D   G

Count: 1   2   3   4   etc.

G   C   D   G

Practice Tips

1. Spend some time playing each new chord by itself. Form the chord with your left hand, play it, then take your hand away and do it all over again. The goal is to be able to form the chords without thinking about where each finger goes.

2. Isolate and practice the chord changes:
   - G–C–G–C
   - C–D–C–D
   - D–G–D–G

The 12-Bar Blues

The standard musical form for the blues is a 12-measure *chord progression*, or series of chords, called the *12-bar blues*. In essence, it consists of three chords (in the *G blues* that follows: G7, C, and D7) and can be heard in hundreds of blues and popular songs. Again, for a crisp sound, try flicking your wrist a little with each strum.

Track 6 *12-Bar Blues*

Practice Tips

1. Spend some time playing each new chord by itself. Form the chord with your left hand, play it, then take your hand away and do it all over again. The goal is to be able to form the chords without thinking about where each finger goes.

2. Isolate and practice the chord changes:
   - G7–C–G7–C
   - G7–D7–G7–D7
   - D7–C–D7–C

Two New Chords and Another 12-Bar Blues

The following five- and six-string chords sound fuller than the four-string chords you've been playing so far. Like the D chord, they involve your first three fingers playing adjacent strings. Stay on your fingertips to keep from muting strings accidentally.

The A Chord

Put your 1st finger on the 2nd fret of the 4th string. Put your 2nd finger on the 2nd fret of the 3rd string. Put your 3rd finger on the 2nd fret of the 2nd string. Strum down over the top five strings.

Note: It's okay if all three fingers aren't right next to the fret for this one; just do the best you can.

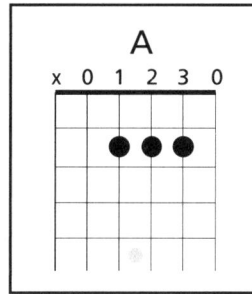

A
x 0 1 2 3 0

The E Chord

Put your 1st finger on the 1st fret of the 3rd string. Put your 2nd finger on the 2nd fret of the 5th string. Put your 3rd finger on the 2nd fret of the 4th string. Strum down over all six strings.

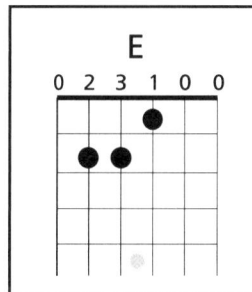

E
0 2 3 1 0 0

Try these new chords in a short tune.

Track 7 *Another Three-Chord Tune*

A   D etc.   E   A

4/4

Count: 1   2   3   4   etc.

12-Bar Blues in A

You may be wondering why the 12-bar blues is showing up again in a section designated as "rock." This is because rock music, especially classic rock, is heavily influenced by the blues.

The blues in A that follows consists of the chords A, D, and E. Be sure to strum down on the top five strings for A, the top four for D, and all six for E. At first, you may need to look down at your right hand while you strum, but eventually you will be able to hit the right number of strings by feel. On the CD, you'll hear an A chord after the final E chord, just to give a sense of finality.

Track 8 *12-Bar Blues in A*

Count: 1   2   3   4   etc.

Tips for Changing Chords

1. To switch from A to D, slide your 3rd finger up one fret on the 2nd string, then move your 1st and 2nd fingers together. To switch back, try the same thing in reverse.

2. To switch from A to E, move your 1st finger from the 2nd fret of the 4th string to the 1st fret of the 3rd string, then move your 2nd and 3rd fingers together.

3. To switch from E to D, slide your 1st finger up one fret on the 3rd string, then move your 2nd and 3rd fingers.

Your Next Two Chords: CMaj7 and Amin7

The C Major 7 Chord

Place your 3rd finger on the 3rd fret of the 5th string. Place your 2nd finger on the 2nd fret of the 4th string. Strum down over the top five strings.

The abbreviation for C Major 7 is CMaj7.

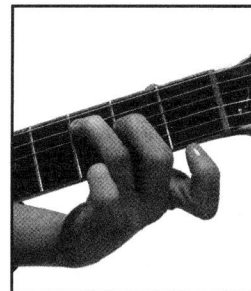

CMaj7
x 3 2 0 0 0

The A Minor 7 Chord

Keep the 2nd finger where it is, lift the 3rd finger off the fretboard, then place the 1st finger on the 1st fret of the 2nd string. Like CMaj7, strum down over the top five strings.

The abbreviation for A Minor 7 is Amin7.

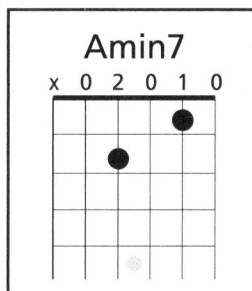

Amin7
x 0 2 0 1 0

Since the 1980s, **Pat Metheny** has been one of the most acclaimed jazz guitarists in the business. He is known for his creativity and willingness to take risks. In 1974, he made his recording debut with Jaco Pastorius, and has since recorded with the likes of Sonny Rollins, Jim Hall, and Herbie Hancock. His recordings with the Pat Metheny Group are difficult to categorize but have secured him a place as one of jazz's great innovators.

J A Z Z

CMaj7-Amin7-Dmin-G7 (or, How to Play 80% of All Jazz Tunes)

Believe it or not, now that you know the four chords mentioned in the chapter title above, you are able to play 80% of all jazz tunes! While this may be a *slight* exaggeration, these four chords are used very frequently, as in the classic-sounding tune below.

Track 9 *Soulful Heart*

Two New Chords: A7 and E7

Next, we have another five-string chord (A7) and another six-string chord (E7). In both of these chords, there is an open string that must ring out between two fretted strings. Make sure that you are on your fingertips to avoid muting the middle string accidentally.

The A7 Chord

Put your 2nd finger on the 2nd fret of the 4th string. Put your 3rd finger on the 2nd fret of the 2nd string. Strum down over the top five strings.

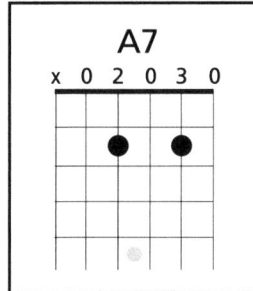

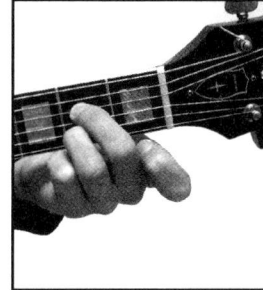

The E7 Chord

Put your 1st finger on the 1st fret of the 3rd string. Put your 2nd finger on the 2nd fret of the 5th string. Strum down over all six strings.

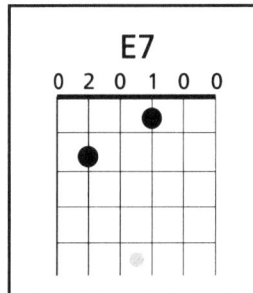

Play the short tune below to practice your new chords.

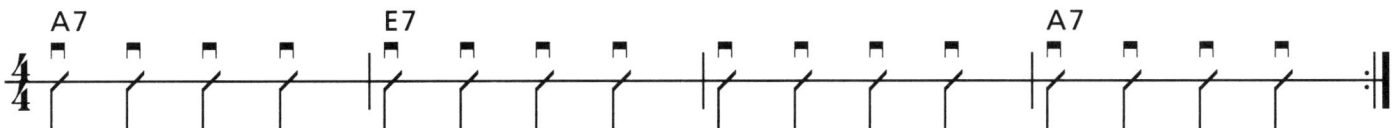

Track 10 *Careful*

Now, you're ready for a version of the 12-bar blues similar to the one on page 22; but instead of using the chords A, D, and E, we'll use A7, D7, and E7. Be sure to strum down on the top five strings for A7, the top four for D7, and all six for E7.

The New Blues

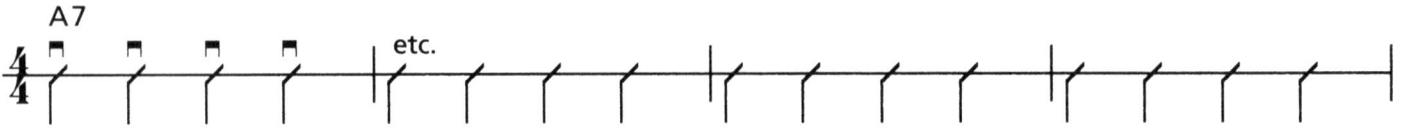

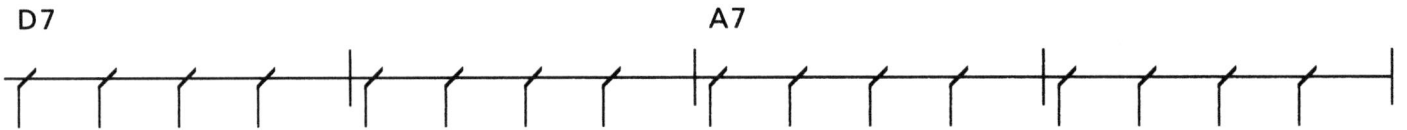

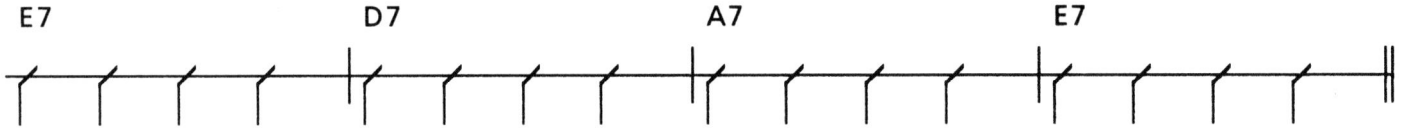

Tips for Changing Chords

1. When changing from A7 to D7, move your 2nd and 3rd fingers simultaneously from the 4th and 2nd strings to the 3rd and 1st strings; both fingers remain at the 2nd fret. Then put your 1st finger on the 1st fret of the 2nd string.

2. When changing from E7 to D7, start with your 1st finger: Move it from the 3rd to the 2nd string, keeping it at the 1st fret.

Basic Rhythm and Strumming

So far, your right hand has stayed constant, strumming down four times every measure while your left hand switches chords. Now, we're going to put your right hand to work, strumming up as well as down.

Quarter Strums Review

You've learned that a beat is a division of time in music, its pulse or heartbeat, and that, in $\frac{4}{4}$ time, there are four beats in a measure. You have been tapping your foot and counting along with the beats: "1, 2, 3, 4." A quarter strum lasts for one beat, so it takes four of them to fill a measure.

Eighth Strums

Now, let's divide each beat in half. Tap your foot, count and clap: "1, 2, 3, 4." Keeping the duration of the beats (and taps of your foot) the same, insert "and" between every number and count and clap: "1–&, 2–&, 3–&, 4–&." See example to the right.

Track 12

```
1    2    3    4

1 & 2 & 3 & 4 &
Onbeats    Offbeats
```

Above is how *eighth rhythms* are counted. The first half of each beat, indicated by the number, is the *onbeat*. The second half, the "&," is the *offbeat*. *Eighth strums* last for one half of a beat, so it takes eight of them to fill a measure.

Let's strum some eighths in the following exercise. Begin counting slowly and evenly: "1–&, 2–&, 3–&, 4–&." Now play an A chord, strumming down ⊓ on the onbeats and up ∨ on the offbeats, while keeping your grip on the pick relatively loose.

Track 13 *Strumming Eighths on A*

A

$\frac{4}{4}$

Count: 1 & 2 & 3 & 4 &   1 & 2 & 3 & 4 &   1 & 2 & 3 & 4 &   1 & 2 & 3 & 4 &

Now, we're going to use down-and-up, or *alternate*, strumming on an entire song. This one is in the style of "Sweet Child O' Mine" by Guns N' Roses. It has the same chords as the 12-bar blues, but in a slightly different order. Take your time and work on playing solid, steady eighth strums with your right hand.

Note: You can use your thumb for alternate strumming, but you may find the upstroke a little difficult. If you haven't used a pick yet, try it now. It'll be tricky at first, but keep at it; a little extra work now will make playing much easier in the future.

Track 14 *Nostalgia*

◇ = Whole strum gets four beats

Triplets

A *triplet* divides a unit of musical time, such as a beat, into three even parts. It is signified by the number "3," which is placed above or below a group of strum symbols. An *eighth triplet* consists of three eighth strums that, together, take up the space of one beat. They are counted like this: "1-&-ah, 2-&-ah," and so on.

To illustrate this, let's look at three different ways that a four-beat measure can be divided (see right). Tap your foot on the onbeats, while clapping and counting the rhythms along with the CD.

Track 15

1. Quarter rhythms

2. Eighth rhythms

3. Triplet rhythms

Swing Eighths

The unique feel of *swing eighths* is created by the use of triplet rhythms. They are strummed on the first and third parts of the beat, the onbeat and the "ah" (see right).

However, they are written and counted as straight eighth strums (1–&, 2–&, etc.). In this book, the swing eighth feel is indicated at the beginning of each tune by the caption: *Swing 8ths.*

Try to play swing eighths on an A7 chord, strumming down on the onbeats and up on the "&s."

Swing 8ths
A7

Track 16

Count: 1 & 2 & 3 & 4 & 1 & 2 & 3 & 4 &

Now, try it on a 12-bar blues.

Track 17 ## Swing Blues

Swing 8ths
A7

etc.

Count: 1 & 2 & 3 & 4 & etc.

D7   A7

E7   D7   A7   E7

Minor Chords and a New Strum

It's time to learn a couple of new minor chords, which, you may have noticed, have a darker sound than either major chords (G, C, D, etc.) or "7" chords (G7, D7, A7, etc.). These minor chords will expand the range of moods we can create on the guitar.

R O C K

The A Minor Chord

Put your 1st finger on the 1st fret of the 2nd string. Put your 2nd finger on the 2nd fret of the 4th string. Put your 3rd finger on the 2nd fret of the 3rd string. Strum down over the highest five strings. Notice that this chord is only one fret away from being an A chord (page 21). The abbreviation for A Minor is Amin.

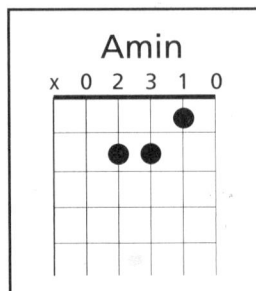

The E Minor Chord

Put your 2nd finger on the 2nd fret of the 5th string. Put your 3rd finger on the 2nd fret of the 4th string. Strum down over all six strings. Notice that this is like an E chord (page 21) but without the 1st finger. The abbreviation for E Minor is Emin.

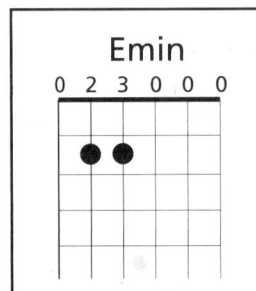

First, let's use the A Minor chord. This song is in the style of Bob Dylan's "Knockin' on Heaven's Door." Try it first with quarter strums, then with eighth strums.

Track 18 — On the Way to Heaven

Combining Quarter and Eighth Strums

This strum pattern combines quarter and eighth rhythms. To start, tap your foot and count a steady: "1, 2, 3, 4." Then divide beats 2 and 4 in half, so you're counting: "1, 2–&, 3, 4–&."

Approach this in the same way as steady eighth strums: Strum down on the onbeats (1, 2, 3, 4) and up on the offbeats (&s) of beats 2 and 4. Your pattern will be: down, down-up, down, down-up.

Let's play this new pattern on an E Minor chord.

Track 19 *E Minor Strum*

Now, let's use the new strum pattern to play a song in the style of The Beatles' "Let It Be." Because there is a lot of switching between chords, don't forget to isolate and practice the chord changes.

Track 20 *Allow It to Happen*

Variations on the 12-Bar Blues

Remember, the blues is based on a 12-measure, three-chord progression. Now, we will learn to create variety within that simple structure with new strumming patterns and ways to change the order of the chords. These variations can add interest to the progressions you already know.

We'll be playing the strum pattern from the previous page (down, down-up, down, down-up), but this time, we'll be using swing eighths (page 29). Let's try this first on a G7 chord.

Swing 8ths

G7

Track 21

Count: 1 2 & 3 4 & 1 2 & 3 4 &

Now, try the pattern in a song. Notice that C is played in the second measure; this breaks up the first four bars and is a common variation on the 12-bar blues.

Track 22 Country Blues

Swing 8ths

G7 **C** etc. **G7**

Count: 1 2 & 3 4 & etc.

C **G7**

D7 **C** **G7**

The Bass-Strum Pattern

Here's another way to make your strumming more interesting. This technique breaks the chords into two parts:

1. The *bass* (lowest) string
2. The remainder of the strings in the chord

Let's start with an A7 chord.

1. Form A7 with your fretting hand.
2. With your right hand, pick the lowest string in the chord (remember, this is a five-string chord, so the lowest string is the 5th string, A).
3. Now strum the rest of the chord—the highest four strings—three times.

This is a four-beat pattern, so it can be played once every measure in $\frac{4}{4}$. It looks like this:

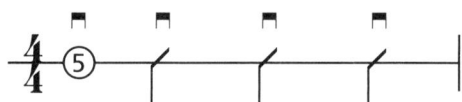

④	= Open 4th string
⑤	= Open 5th string
⑥	= Open 6th string

Let's look at two other chords:

- D7: Pick the bass (4th) string, then strum the remaining three strings three times.

- E7: Pick the bass (6th) string, then strum the remaining strings three times.

Here is a blues tune using the bass-strum technique.

Track 23 *Bass-Strum Blues*

Minor Blues

In this chapter, we're going to use minor chords to play another variation of the blues, but first, we need to learn a new chord: E Minor 7, or Emin7.

The E Minor 7 Chord

Put your 2nd finger on the 2nd fret of the 5th string. Strum all six strings. Notice that this is one note away from being an E7 chord.

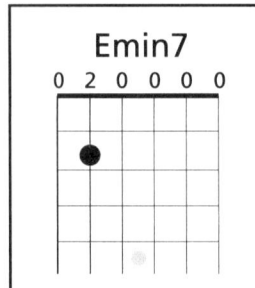

Emin7
0 2 0 0 0 0

Let's practice Emin7 in the exercise below, along with two other minor chords you've already learned (Amin7 and Dmin). When you are comfortable, replace the quarter strums with swing eighth strums.

Track 24 *A Minor Song*

| Amin7 | | | | Dmin | | | | Emin7 | | | | Amin7 | | | |

One of the most influential and immediately identifiable electric guitarists of all time, **B. B. King** has been making music since the 1940s. In 1969, King was catapulted into mainstream stardom with his recording of the minor blues tune "The Thrill Is Gone." He continues to tour and has recorded with contemporary artists such as Eric Clapton and U2.

PHOTO BY TAD HERSHORN

Now you're ready to play a *minor blues*, which is a 12-bar blues in which all the chords are minor (notice the more introspective mood that is created). Use the example below to practice all the different strumming patterns: quarter strums, *straight eighth* (eighth strums that are not swung) and swing eighth strums, the quarter and eighth strum combination, and the bass-strum pattern.

Track 25 *Minor Blues*

Amin7 Dmin Amin7

Dmin Amin7

Emin7 Dmin Amin7

Tip for Changing Chords

When changing from Amin7 to Dmin, move your 1st and 2nd fingers simultaneously; they go over one string each (from the 2nd and 4th strings to the 1st and 3rd strings) and stay on the same frets.

Reading Tablature

Tablature, also known as TAB, is a graphic way of writing guitar music. It is read differently than *standard music notation*, which we will explore later.

Tablature consists of six lines, each line representing a string of the guitar.

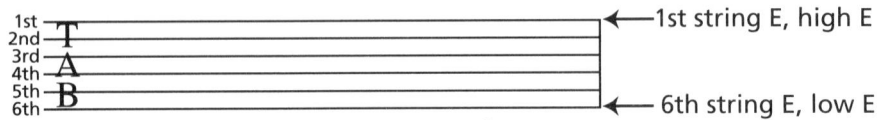

```
1st ─┬T──────────────────────────────────  ◄──1st string E, high E
2nd ─┤────────────────────────────────────
3rd ─┤A───────────────────────────────────
4th ─┤────────────────────────────────────
5th ─┤B───────────────────────────────────
6th ─┴────────────────────────────────────  ◄── 6th string E, low E
```

The numbers on the lines represent the frets to be played. In other words, if there's a "2" on the third line down, play the 2nd fret on the 3rd string. If two numbers are stacked on top of each other—such as "0" (meaning open) on the 5th string and "2" on the 4th string—play them at the same time. Here are a few examples you can try:

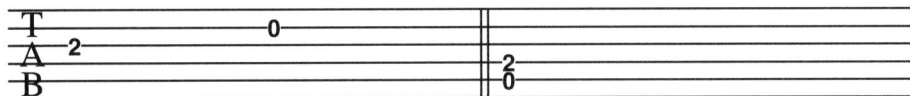

```
T──────────────────0──────────╫────────────────
A─2───────────────────────────╫────────────────
B─────────────────────────────╫─2──────────────
                              ║ 0
```

3rd string, 2nd fret	2nd string, open	4th string, 2nd fret 5th string, open *Play both at the same time by strumming*

The numbers underneath the lines show you which left-hand fingers to use. Here are some more examples:

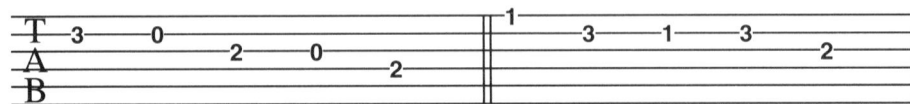

```
T─3───0────────────────────╫─1──────────────────────────
A───────2───0──────────────╫────3────1────3──────────────
B──────────────2───────────╫─────────────────2──────────
```

3   0   2   0   2   1   3   1   3   2

↖ Left-hand fingers

Tablature Exercise

Write the location of each note shown in TAB, then play each note. The correct answers are on the bottom of page 38.

```
T--2---------------|------------------|------1-----------|------------------|
A------------------|--2---------------|-----------------|------------------|
B------------------|------------------|-----------------|--3---------------|
```

```
_____ string      _____ string      _____ string      _____ string
_____ fret        _____ fret        _____ fret         _____ fret
```

```
T------------------|--3---------------|------3-----------|--0---------------|
A--2---------------|------------------|-----------------|------------------|
B------------------|------------------|-----------------|------------------|
```

```
_____ string      _____ string      _____ string      _____ string
_____ fret        _____ fret        _____ fret         _____ fret
```

Now that you know how to read TAB, you're ready to try a *melody* (a succession of single tones that comprise the tune of a song). In tablature, notes are written from left to right in the order they are played. Below, rhythm is indicated above the fret numbers with dots, which represent short tones, and lines, which represent long tones. Play through the familiar tune below.

• = Short note
— = Long note

Track 26 *Yankee Doodle*

```
T--1---1---3---0---|--1-------0---3---|--1---1---3---0---|--1-------0-------|
A-----------------0|------------------|-----------------|------------------|
B------------------|------------------|-----------------|------------------|
   1   1   3   0      1   0   3   0      1   1   3   0      1       0
```

```
T--1---1---3---0---|-1----0-----------|-0---------------0|-1--------1-------|
A-----------------0|---------3---1----|-----0---2--------|------------------|
B------------------|------------------|-----------------|------------------|
   1   1   3   0      1   0   3   1      0   0   2   0      1       1
```

Track 27 *Twinkle, Twinkle, Little Star*

```
T----------3---3---|--0---0-------3---|-1---1---0---0----|------------------|
A--0---0-----------|------------------|-----------------|--2---2---0-------|
B------------------|------------------|-----------------|------------------|
   0   0   3   3      0   0       3      1   1   0   0      2   2   0
```

```
T--3---3---1---1---|--0---0-----------|-3---3---1---1----|--0---0-----------|
A------------------|----------2-------|-----------------|----------2-------|
B------------------|------------------|-----------------|------------------|
   3   3   1   1      0   0   2          3   3   1   1      0   0   2
```

Here is another well-known melody for you to practice reading tablature.

Track 28 *I've Been Working on the Railroad*

Answers: Page 37

An Introduction to Rock Playing

Now that you've learned some basics, it's time to play some things that sound a little more like rock music.

Power Chords

Power chords are essential to rock guitarists. These two-string "chords"* are very popular in rock and blues because of their simplicity and heavy sound. They are denoted by a "5" placed next to a chord letter (for example, "A5").

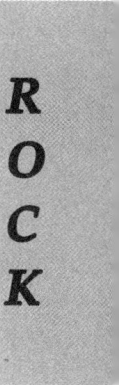

The A5 Chord

The two tones of the power chord come directly from the chords you already know. Try this: simultaneously play the lowest two tones of an A chord—the open 5th string and the 4th string, 2nd fret with your 1st finger. You just played an A power chord. If you have an electric guitar, turn it up loud and let your A5 ring.

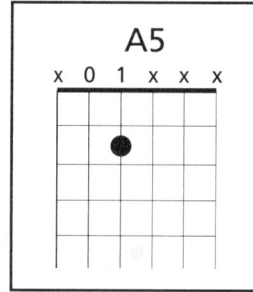

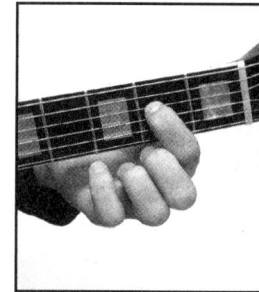

A5
x 0 1 x x x

The D5 Chord

Again, play the lowest two notes in a D chord: the open 4th string and the 3rd string, 2nd fret with your 1st finger.

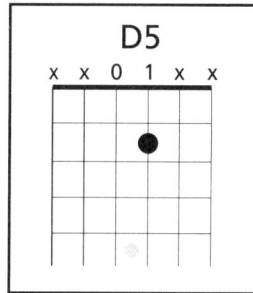

D5
x x 0 1 x x

The E5 Chord

The lowest two pitches are the same as the E chord, but the fingering is a little different. Play the open 6th string and use your 1st finger to play the 5th string, 2nd fret.

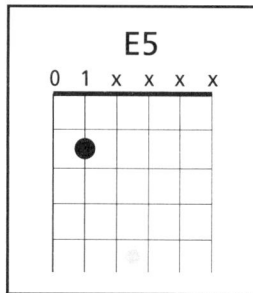

E5
0 1 x x x x

Play this short example in eighth rhythms using all downstrokes. Be sure to strike only the two strings of each power chord.

Track 29 *Power Chord Exercise*

A5	D5	A5	E5
⊓ ⊓ ⊓ ⊓ ⊓ ⊓ ⊓ ⊓ ⊓ etc.			

```
T
A--2-2-2-2-2-2-2-2----2-2-2-2-2-2-2-2----2-2-2-2-2-2-2-2-------------------------
B--0-0-0-0-0-0-0-0----0-0-0-0-0-0-0-0----0-0-0-0-0-0-0-0----2-2-2-2-2-2-2-2------
                                                           0-0-0-0-0-0-0-0------

   1 1 1 1 1 1 1 1     1 1 1 1 1 1 1 1     1 1 1 1 1 1 1 1    1 1 1 1 1 1 1 1
   0 0 0 0 0 0 0 0     0 0 0 0 0 0 0 0     0 0 0 0 0 0 0 0    0 0 0 0 0 0 0 0
```

A New 12-Bar Blues

Now we're going to tweak those power chords and use them to make a cool-sounding pattern for the 12-bar blues. Various forms of this pattern can be heard in countless rock songs such as "Come Together" (The Beatles), "Rock and Roll" (Led Zeppelin), and "Truckin'" (Grateful Dead).

To start, play an A5. Now—keeping your 1st finger down—put your 3rd or 4th finger (whichever is more comfortable) on the 4th fret of the 4th string and play that along with the open 5th string. Alternate between these two chords, playing each one twice.

The other two chords in this 12-bar blues work the same way:

- Play a D5. Keep the 4th string open and alternate between the 2nd and 4th frets on the 3rd string.

- Play an E5. Keep the 6th string open and alternate between the 2nd and 4th frets on the 5th string.

R
O
C
K

Here it is in tablature. Remember to use all downstrokes.

Track 30 — Rock Blues

A5

```
  ⊓ ⊓ ⊓ ⊓ ⊓ ⊓ ⊓ ⊓   etc.
T|------------------|------------------|------------------|------------------|
A|-2-2-4-4-2-2-4-4--|-2-2-4-4-2-2-4-4--|-2-2-4-4-2-2-4-4--|-2-2-4-4-2-2-4-4--|
B|-0-0-0-0-0-0-0-0--|-0-0-0-0-0-0-0-0--|-0-0-0-0-0-0-0-0--|-0-0-0-0-0-0-0-0--|

  1 1 3 3 1 1 3 3    1 1 3 3 1 1 3 3    1 1 3 3 1 1 3 3    1 1 3 3 1 1 3 3
  0 0 0 0 0 0 0 0    0 0 0 0 0 0 0 0    0 0 0 0 0 0 0 0    0 0 0 0 0 0 0 0
```

D5   **A5**

```
T|------------------|------------------|------------------|------------------|
A|-2-2-4-4-2-2-4-4--|-2-2-4-4-2-2-4-4--|------------------|------------------|
B|-0-0-0-0-0-0-0-0--|-0-0-0-0-0-0-0-0--|-2-2-4-4-2-2-4-4--|-2-2-4-4-2-2-4-4--|
                                       |-0-0-0-0-0-0-0-0--|-0-0-0-0-0-0-0-0--|

  1 1 3 3 1 1 3 3    1 1 3 3 1 1 3 3    1 1 3 3 1 1 3 3    1 1 3 3 1 1 3 3
  0 0 0 0 0 0 0 0    0 0 0 0 0 0 0 0    0 0 0 0 0 0 0 0    0 0 0 0 0 0 0 0
```

E5   **D5**   **A5**   **E5**

```
T|------------------|------------------|------------------|------------------|
A|------------------|-2-2-4-4-2-2-4-4--|------------------|------------------|
B|-2-2-4-4-2-2-4-4--|-0-0-0-0-0-0-0-0--|-2-2-4-4-2-2-4-4--|-2-2-4-4-2-2-4-4--|
 |-0-0-0-0-0-0-0-0--|                  |-0-0-0-0-0-0-0-0--|-0-0-0-0-0-0-0-0--|

  1 1 3 3 1 1 3 3    1 1 3 3 1 1 3 3    1 1 3 3 1 1 3 3    1 1 3 3 1 1 3 3
  0 0 0 0 0 0 0 0    0 0 0 0 0 0 0 0    0 0 0 0 0 0 0 0    0 0 0 0 0 0 0 0
```

Rock Riffs

A *riff* is a short, repeated musical idea. In rock music, a riff is often the foundation of an entire song. When you think of Black Sabbath's "Iron Man" or Led Zeppelin's "Whole Lotta Love," the riffs are probably what first come to mind.

Try the following riff. Remember, with the tablature in this book, the pitches with dots above them are short in duration and the ones with dashes are long. Pay attention to the left-hand fingering underneath each tone—it's there to make the example easier for you.

Track 31 Rock Riff 1

The next riff is a little more involved. Turn it up and play it with lots of attitude.

Track 32 Rock Riff 2

Power Chords and the Blues

One of the great things about the blues is the way you can get a big, rocking sound by playing something very basic. Below, we'll use power chords to play a blues progression (like we did in the previous rock section), but this time, we'll do it using swing eighths. Play the first example using only downstrokes. With contained movements of your wrist, pick only the strings that are called for.

Track 33 *Simple Shuffle*

Swing 8ths

```
A5                      D5                      A5                      E5
⊓ ⊓ ⊓ ⊓ ⊓ ⊓ ⊓ ⊓         etc.
T
A  2 2 2 2 2 2 2 2       2 2 2 2 2 2 2 2         2 2 2 2 2 2 2 2
B  0 0 0 0 0 0 0 0       0 0 0 0 0 0 0 0                                 2 2 2 2 2 2 2 2
                                                 0 0 0 0 0 0 0 0         0 0 0 0 0 0 0 0

   1 1 1 1 1 1 1 1       1 1 1 1 1 1 1 1         1 1 1 1 1 1 1 1         1 1 1 1 1 1 1 1
   0 0 0 0 0 0 0 0       0 0 0 0 0 0 0 0         0 0 0 0 0 0 0 0         0 0 0 0 0 0 0 0
```

Now we're going to tweak those power chords and use them to make a cool-sounding pattern for the 12-bar blues. This pattern can be heard in the playing of pioneer artists such as Robert Johnson and in such recent artists as Kenny Wayne Shepherd.

The following blues progression is exactly the same as the one on page 40, but here, we'll be using swing eighths. Be sure to listen to the CD for the correct way to play this.

Track 34 *Shufflin'*

Swing 8ths

```
A5
⊓ ⊓ ⊓ ⊓ ⊓ ⊓ ⊓ ⊓         etc.
T
A  2 2 4 4 2 2 4 4       2 2 4 4 2 2 4 4         2 2 4 4 2 2 4 4         2 2 4 4 2 2 4 4
B  0 0 0 0 0 0 0 0       0 0 0 0 0 0 0 0         0 0 0 0 0 0 0 0         0 0 0 0 0 0 0 0

   1 1 3 3 1 1 3 3       1 1 3 3 1 1 3 3         1 1 3 3 1 1 3 3         1 1 3 3 1 1 3 3
   0 0 0 0 0 0 0 0       0 0 0 0 0 0 0 0         0 0 0 0 0 0 0 0         0 0 0 0 0 0 0 0

D5                                              A5
T
A  2 2 4 4 2 2 4 4       2 2 4 4 2 2 4 4
B  0 0 0 0 0 0 0 0       0 0 0 0 0 0 0 0         2 2 4 4 2 2 4 4         2 2 4 4 2 2 4 4
                                                0 0 0 0 0 0 0 0         0 0 0 0 0 0 0 0

   1 1 3 3 1 1 3 3       1 1 3 3 1 1 3 3         1 1 3 3 1 1 3 3         1 1 3 3 1 1 3 3
   0 0 0 0 0 0 0 0       0 0 0 0 0 0 0 0         0 0 0 0 0 0 0 0         0 0 0 0 0 0 0 0

E5                      D5                      A5                      E5
T
A
B  2 2 4 4 2 2 4 4       2 2 4 4 2 2 4 4         2 2 4 4 2 2 4 4         2 2 4 4 2 2 4 4
   0 0 0 0 0 0 0 0       0 0 0 0 0 0 0 0         0 0 0 0 0 0 0 0         0 0 0 0 0 0 0 0

   1 1 3 3 1 1 3 3       1 1 3 3 1 1 3 3         1 1 3 3 1 1 3 3         1 1 3 3 1 1 3 3
   0 0 0 0 0 0 0 0       0 0 0 0 0 0 0 0         0 0 0 0 0 0 0 0         0 0 0 0 0 0 0 0
```

A Word About Improvisation

Keep It Simple

There is no rule saying that to play jazz you have to create complex solos with flurries of notes. Quite the contrary: jazz masters such as trumpeter Miles Davis and saxophonist Sonny Rollins have composed entire solos around only one note!

Many people avoid playing jazz because they think it's "too difficult." This is a myth. Jazz can be very complex, but its foundations are very simple. Listening to the music of jazz musicians (like Davis and Rollins) who express themselves simply, yet authoritatively, can help you understand this.

Following is a solo made up entirely of two notes, both of which are on the 1st string. Play it along with the CD, then use it as a springboard for your own ideas. After the solo is played once, you will have the opportunity to improvise a solo of your own as the band plays through the tune three more times. You can play the two notes any way you'd like. Experiment. Listen to the notes as you play them. Do not judge what you are playing! Let yourself be creative. Have fun with it—you can even allow yourself to be silly. If there's one thing that jazz definitely has, it's a sense of humor.

Track 35 *E String Jam*

These chord symbols are for your teacher or friends to play along with you.

Reading Standard Music Notation

Like tablature, *standard music notation* is a way of writing music on a set of lines (five rather than six) and indicates which pitches to play in what order. There are, however, two big differences: 1) Standard music notation tells you what pitches to play, but not where to play them. 2) Standard music notation tells you the exact duration of each pitch, not an estimate.

Pitch

Remember that pitch refers to the degree of highness or lowness of a musical tone. The first aspect of standard music notation we will cover deals with how we know which pitch to play.

Staff

A *staff* consists of five lines and four spaces. Music will be written on these lines and spaces.

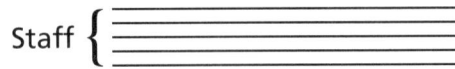

Staff

Clef

A *clef* is a symbol which tells us which pitches are represented by which lines and which spaces. Guitarists read the *treble clef* 𝄞, also known as the *G clef*. It is called the G clef because it surrounds the line called G. In treble clef, the second line is G.

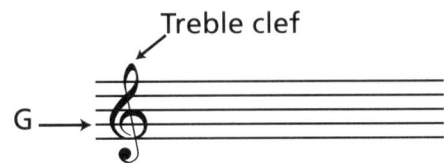

Treble clef

G

The *musical alphabet* consists of seven letters: A, B, C, D, E, F, G. Each line and space of the staff represents one of these letters. By placing *notes* 𝅗𝅥 on these lines and spaces, musical pitch is indicated.

To the right are the notes on the lines. To remember them, use this phrase: **E**very **G**ood **B**oy **D**oes **F**ine.

Notes on the Lines

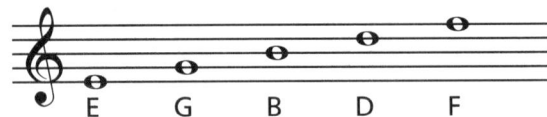

E G B D F

To the right are the notes in the spaces. To remember these, think of the word FACE.

Notes in the Spaces

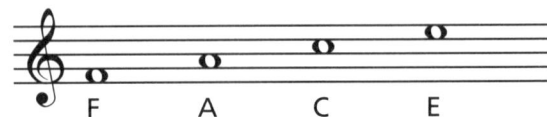

F A C E

In the exercise below, write the names of the notes on the spaces underneath them. You will see there are enough letters in the musical alphabet to spell many different words. (Answers: bottom of page 57.)

Exercise 1

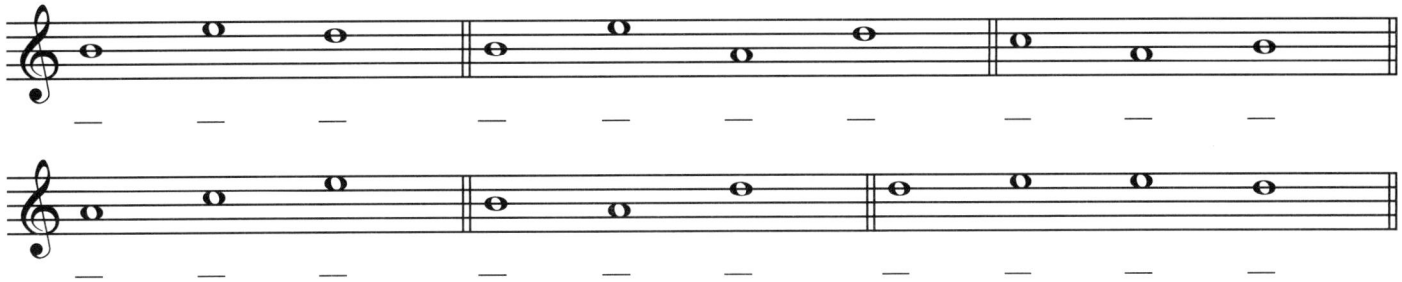

See if you can name all the notes below without looking at page 44. Remember that the notes proceed alphabetically; for example, if the note in a space is A, the note on the next line up has to be B. (Answers: bottom of page 57.)

Exercise 2

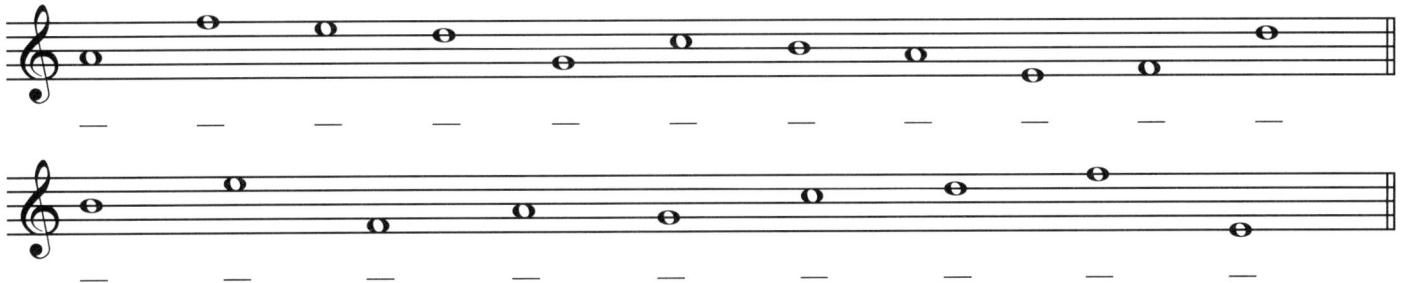

Rhythm in Standard Notation

Recall that rhythm is created by the arrangement of long and short sounds and silences. This is the aspect of standard notation that tells us the duration of the notes we are playing.

Time Signature Review

A time signature tells us how to count the music. Most popular music is counted in groups of four, but this is not always the case.

A time signature has two numbers, one stacked on top of the other.

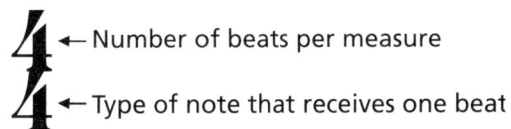

← Number of beats per measure
← Type of note that receives one beat

Parts of a Note

The appearance of a particular note indicates how long it will last. By the use of *heads, stems,* and *flags, note value* (duration of a note) is communicated.

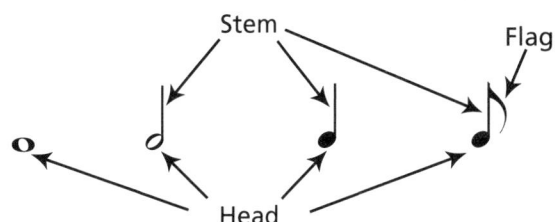

Stem   Flag

Head

Notes on the 1st String

Now, it's time to transfer the notes from the page to the guitar. You'll be reading standard music notation on the first four frets. The fret numbers will correspond to the left-hand fingers you will use to fret the notes (play all notes on the 1st fret with your 1st finger, notes on the 2nd fret with your 2nd finger, etc.).

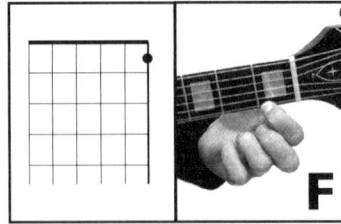

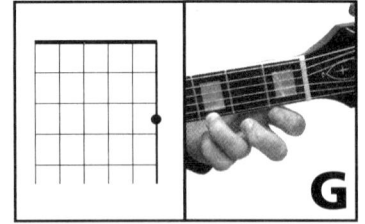

Quarter Notes 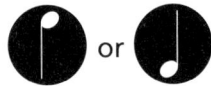 or

A *quarter note* is solid and has a stem. It is held for one beat. Four of them would fill a four-beat measure. Notes on or above the middle line of the staff have the stems going down. Notes below the middle line have the stems going up.

The following two exercises are in $\frac{4}{4}$, which means there are four beats per measure. Count: "1, 2, 3, 4; 1, 2, 3, 4," etc., tapping your foot once for each beat. Since a quarter note lasts for one beat, you will be playing one note for each tap. Keep the speed, or *tempo,* of the exercises steady. Start slowly at first and practice until you don't have to think about where the notes are.

Track 36 *1st String Exercise—No. 1*

Count: 1 2 3 4 1 2 3 4 1 2 3 4 1 2 3 4

```
T--0--0--3--0--|--3--1--0--1--|--3--0--1--1--|--0--3--0--0--
A
B
```

0 0 3 0   3 1 0 1   3 0 1 1   0 3 0 0

1st String Exercise — No. 2

(music notation and TAB)

0 0 3 3   0 3 1 1   3 0 1 1   0 1 0 0

Whole Notes

A *whole note* is hollow and without a stem. It lasts for four beats (an entire measure in $\frac{4}{4}$ time).

Whole Rests

A *rest* is a symbol used to indicate silence in music. A *whole rest*, which looks like an upside-down hat, signifies four beats of silence.

A Note About Rests

It is important to create silence for a rest by stopping the strings from vibrating. This is best accomplished by using the heel of your right hand.

Now let's try the notes on the 1st string using whole notes and rests.

The Whole Truth

(music notation and TAB)

Count: 1 2 3 4   1 2 3 4   etc.

0   1   3   1   0   3   0

Notice below that the counting numbers for rests are shown in parentheses.

...And Nothing But

(music notation and TAB)

Count: 1 2 3 4   (1 2 3 4)   etc.

1   0   3   1   3   0

Notes on the 2nd String

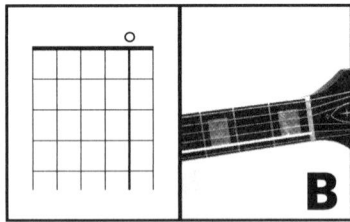

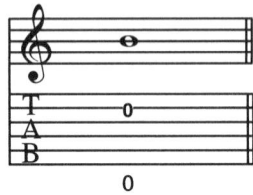

B

0

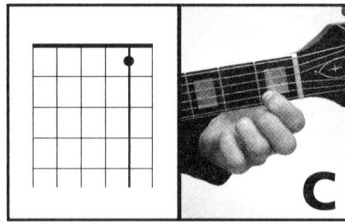

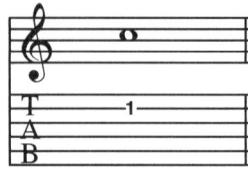

C

1

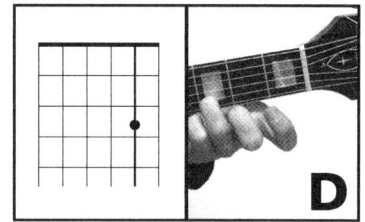

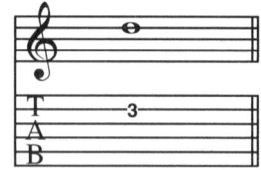

D

3

Half Notes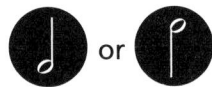

A *half note* is hollow and has a stem. It is held for two beats. Two of them would fill a four-beat measure. If you play a half note on beat 1 of a measure, you would hold it through beat 2 and play the next note on beat 3 (see right).

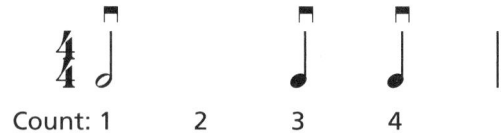

Count: 1　　2　　3　　4

Quarter Rests

A *quarter rest,* like the quarter note, lasts for one beat. If there is a quarter rest on beat 3 of a measure, stop the strings on beat 3 and wait until beat 4 to play (see example to the right).

Stop string

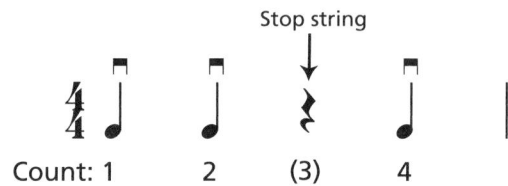

Count: 1　　2　　(3)　　4

Try the example below using your new rhythms and notes.

Track 40 *I've Been Told*

48　The Total Beginning Guitarist

I've Been Told Some More

Count: 1 2 3 4 1 2 3 (4) 1 2 3 4 1 2 3 4

Half Rests

A *half rest,* which resembles a hat (right side up), signifies two beats of silence.

In the following two pieces, the rhythm is created by an arrangement of half notes and half rests.

Two-Step Shuffle

Count: 1 2 3 4   1 2 (3 4)   etc.

Shave and a Haircut...

Below are two more songs on the first two strings. Most of the notes and note values you've learned so far will be featured in these songs. Remember to keep your tempo steady and not to rush.

Track 44 *Open Hands*

Track 45 *High Lonesome*

Notes on the 3rd String

We have only two notes to learn on the 3rd string.

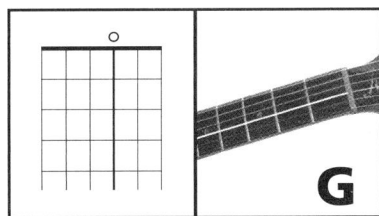

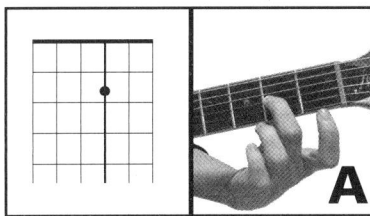

Let's try a couple of tunes using the notes on the 3rd string.

Track 46 Four, No More

Count: 1 2 3 (4) 1 (2) 3 (4)   etc.

0 0 0   2 0   0 0 2 0   0 2 2 0 2   2 0 2 0   2 0   0 0

Track 47 Rest Easy

0 0   0   0 2 0   2   2 0   2 0   2 0   0 0

Eighth Notes ♪ or ♪

An *eighth note* is solid and has a stem and flag. It lasts for half a beat. Eight of them are required to fill a four-beat measure.

Every beat can be divided in half by counting: "1–&, 2–&, 3–&, 4–&" (& = "and"). As we learned with eighth rhythms, the numbers are the onbeats and the "&s" are the offbeats. When tapping the beats, bring your foot down 👞 on the onbeats and up 👟 on the offbeats.

Eighth notes are to be picked in the same way that eighth rhythms are strummed: pick down ⊓ on the onbeats (as your foot is tapping downward) and pick up V on the offbeats (as your foot is coming up).

When eighth notes appear in groups, their flags are *beamed* together either in fours or twos.

1 & 2 &	3 & 4 &
Sometimes they are grouped in fours	Sometimes they are grouped in twos

Now, let's try an exercise with these eighth-note rhythms.

Track 48 ## 3rd String Exercise

Count: 1 & 2 & 3 & 4 &   1 & 2 & 3 & 4 &   1 & 2 & 3 & 4 &   1 & 2 & 3 & (4 &)

```
T
A   0  0  2  2  0  2  0  0 │ 2  0  0  2  2     0  2 │ 2     0     2  2  2 │ 2     0     2
B
```

0 0 2 2 0 2 0 0   2 0 0 2 2   0 2   2   0   2 2 2   2   0   2

The next two songs feature most of the notes and rhythms you've learned so far.

Track 49 *Nappin'*

Track 50 *Eighth-Note Rock*

R
O
C
K

Notes on the 4th String

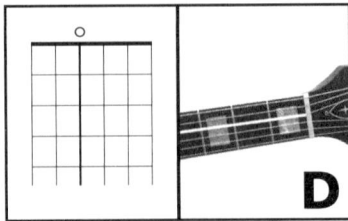

D
0

E
2

F
3

Ties

A *tie* is a curved line that connects two notes of the same pitch. It extends the value of the first note by the value of the second. Do this by picking the note and letting it ring for the duration that includes the two notes together. For example, a quarter note tied to another quarter note lasts for two beats.

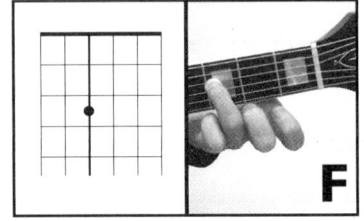

Notice that tied notes in TAB are shown in parentheses.

Track 51 *Along the Road*

Do not pick

Count: 1 2 3 4 1 2 3 4 1 2 3 4 1 2 3 4

0 2 0 3 0 2 0 3 0 3

5

1 2 3 4 1 2 3 4 1 2 3 4 1 2 3 4

0 2 3 2 0 3 0

Up the Road

Count: (1) 2 3 4 | 1 2 3 4 | (1) 2 3 4 | 1 2 3 4

TAB:
0   0 | (0) 0   0 | 0   0 | (0) 0   0
  3 | 3 | 3 | 3
0 3 0 | 0 3 0 | 0 3 0 | 0 3 0

5

(1) 2 3 4 | 1 2 3 4 | 1 2 3 4 | 1 2 3 4

TAB:
0   0 | (0) 0   0 | 0   0 | (0)
  3 | 3 | 3 |
0 3 0 | 0 3 0 | 0 3 0 |

Eighth Rests 𝄾

An *eighth rest* indicates a half beat of silence.

Spang-Spang-a-Lang

Count: 1 & 2 & (3 &) 4 & | 1 & (2) & 3 & (4) & | etc.

TAB:
0 0 2 3   3 2 | 0 2   3 2 2   0 | 0   0 2 2 3 3 | 2 3 2 3 2 0   0

0 0 2 3   3 2   0 2   3 2 2   0   0   0 2 2 3 3   2 3 2 3 2 0   0

Notice that the following melody starts on the offbeat.

Five, Six, Seven, Eight

TAB:
0 2 3   0 3 2 | 2   3 2 3   3 | 0 0   0 0 0 2 0 | 0 3 2 0 2 0 2 0

0 2 3   0 3 2   2   3 2 3   3   0 0   0 0 0 2 0   0 3 2 0 2 0 2 0

Dotted Half Notes 𝅗𝅥. or ♩.

A *dot* that follows a note increases the note's value by one half. A half note is two beats long. Half the value of two is one. Add these two values together and you get three beats (2 + 1 = 3). A *dotted half note* lasts for three beats, the same value as a half note tied to a quarter note.

$$𝅗𝅥. = 𝅗𝅥 \ ♩$$
$$3 = 2 + 1$$

If you find the rhythms in the following song difficult, count and clap them out loud until they feel comfortable. For example, if you see this rhythm...

𝄞 4/4 ♩ ♫ 𝅗𝅥 | 𝅗𝅥 ♩ ♫ ‖
1 & 2 & 3 & 4 & 1 & 2 & 3 & 4 &

...tap your foot on the onbeats (1, 2, 3, 4); count: "1–&, 2–&, 3–&, 4–&; 1–&, 2–&, 3–&, 4–&," and clap the rhythm that is indicated. This may be a little challenging at first but is well worth the effort.

Track 55 *Caveman*

Here's a blues tune that features ties, dotted notes, and
notes on the 4th string.

Track 56 *Blues Solo*

Answers: page 45

Exercise 2

Exercise 1

Notes on the 5th String

Notice that these notes are not touching the staff at all. Because they are too low to appear on the staff, they are written on *ledger lines*. A ledger line is simply an extension of the staff. As the notes get lower, the number of ledger lines increases.

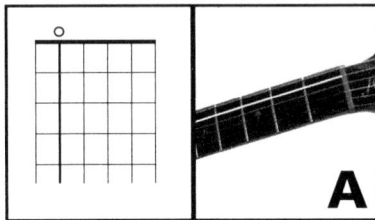

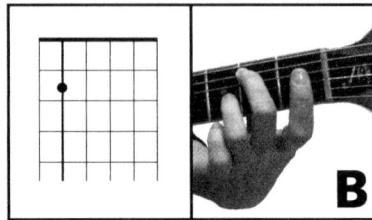

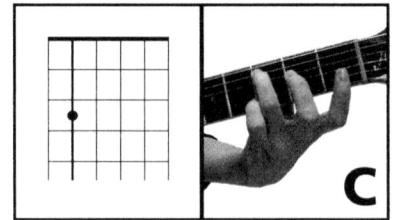

Let's try a couple of exercises using these new notes.

Track 57 *Song for Fonzie*

Track 58 *Song for Whole and Half*

Pickup Notes

Pickup notes precede the first full measure of a song. They make up a short, incomplete measure that leads you into the tune. When there is a pickup note, the last measure of the song will also be incomplete, making up for the notes missing from the pickup measure.

Track 59 — *Riffin' on the 5th*

Pickup notes

Count: 4 & 1 (2 3) 4 etc.

Incomplete measure

Count: 1 2 3

Track 60 — *St. Louis Blues*

Swing 8ths

Amin — E7

Count: 4 & 1 2 3 4 etc.

E7 — Amin

Count: 1 2 3

Accidentals

Accidentals are symbols placed before a note that alter its pitch and location on your instrument. An accidental changes a note for the remainder of the measure in which it is found. Until now, the notes we have been playing are *natural*—they are unaltered by either *sharps* or *flats*.

Sharps

A sharp raises a note by a *half step*, or one fret. For example, high F is on the 1st fret of the 1st string, so F-sharp is on the 2nd fret.

Flats

A flat lowers a note by a half step, or one fret. For example, low B is on the 2nd fret of the 5th string, so B-flat is on the 1st fret.

Naturals

A natural sign cancels out any accidental, thereby restoring the note to its original pitch. For example, F♯ is played on the 2nd fret of the 1st string, and a natural sign restores F to the 1st fret.

In the following exercise, notice that the second note (F♯) is played with the 4th finger. Play slowly at first, until this is comfortable.

Track 61 *Accidental Exercise*

The following exercise demonstrates the use of sharps, flats, and naturals. Notice that the first note in the second measure (D#) is played with the 4th finger. Play slowly at first, until this is comfortable.

Track 62   *12-Tone Tune*

Enharmonics Equivalents

Enharmonic equivalents are notes of the same pitch that are "spelled" in different ways. For example, an F#—which is a half step higher than F—sounds the same and is played on the same string and fret as G♭, which is a half step lower than G.

Below is a list of enharmonic equivalents:

A# = B♭

C# = D♭

D# = E♭

F# = G♭

G# = A♭

Notes on the 6th String

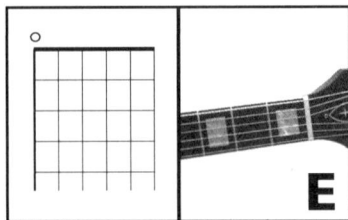

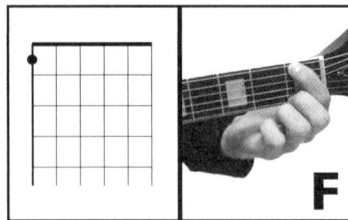

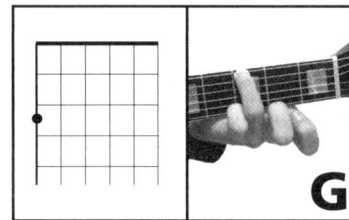

The next song consists almost entirely of eighth notes. Remember to pick down on the onbeats and up on the offbeats.

Track 63 *Baby*

Count: 1 & 2 & 3 & 4 & etc.

```
T
A
B   0   0   1   0   3   0   1   0       0   0   1   0   3   0   1   0
    0   0   1   0   3   0   1   0       0   0   1   0   3   0   1   0
```

```
3
T
A       2       0                   2       0
B   0   0   1   0   3   0   1   0   2   0   2   0   3   0   0
    0   0   1   0   3   0   1   0                   3   0   0
```

Here's another 6th-string exercise to try.

Track 64 *Bass Is the Place*

| Count: | 1 | 2 | 3 | (4) | 1 | 2 | 3 | & | 4 | & | 1 | 2 | 3 | 4 | 1 | & | 2 | & | 3 | (4) |

The rhythm in the following tune is "funky" because ties, rests, and eighth/quarter combinations are used to shift the emphasis to offbeats. This is called *syncopation*.

Track 65 *Funky*

| Count: | 1 | & | 2 | & | (3) | & | 4 | & | 1 | 2 | 3 | 4 | 1 | & | 2 | & | 3 | & | 4 | & | 1 | & | 2 | & | 3 | & | 4 | & |

Make sure you isolate the parts of this song that give you trouble, practicing them over and over until they are more comfortable. Then try them again in the context of the song; they should feel a lot better.

Riff Rock

R O C K

Below is a 12-bar blues, and it is the first tune you will be reading on all six strings. Notice the bluesy sound created when certain notes are flatted. Again, make sure you isolate and practice the parts that give you trouble.

In the first four measures on the CD, you will hear a musical device called *stop-time*. This is where the rhythm section plays only on certain beats of the measure. In measures 1 and 2, they play only on the *downbeats* (a downbeat is the first beat of a measure). In measures 3 and 4, they play on the other beats, but in a way that builds toward the regular accompaniment.

Track 67 *Stop-Time*

Improvising a Solo

J
A
Z
Z

Learning to *improvise* (spontaneously create melodies) on the guitar is a lot like moving to a new town: you explore the area, find the local amenities (dry cleaner, grocery store, etc.), and talk to your new neighbors. Musically speaking, this translates into:

1. Learning the notes on one string

2. Learning the notes on another string

3. Putting the strings together to say something

The key is to be comfortable enough with the notes to string them together into a musical statement, or solo. The *rhythm section* (guitar, bass, and drums) *accompanies*, or backs up, your solo. They listen to every note you play and provide a context for your musical statements. Following the analogy above, the rhythm section is the environment of your new town, as well as new neighbors with whom you are having a conversation.

Improvising on the 1st and 2nd Strings

Let's improvise using the notes on the 1st and 2nd strings. To review, the notes on the 1st string are:

The notes on the 2nd string are:

Below is a typical solo on the 1st and 2nd strings. The rhythm section will accompany the solo with the chords written above the staff. It is important to play the rhythms of the solo correctly—they must coincide with the chord changes to create the intended sound. Remember, you can do a lot with only a few notes. You will have four open *choruses* (a chorus is one time through the tune) to play over.

Track 68 · *A One and-a Two and-a*

Swing 8ths

Note About Jazz Rhythm

Ever wonder why jazz sounds so...jazzy? One of the reasons is something called *swing*. The swing feel is created by the use of swing eighths (they're not just for playing the blues!). Be sure to listen to the accompanying CD, and as many jazz recordings as you can, to really get the feel of how swing is supposed to be played.

Improvising on the 3rd and 4th Strings

Let's review the notes on the 3rd string.

Here are the notes on the 4th string.

After playing along with the following example as written,
you will have four open choruses to improvise over.

Track 69 *Song for Ewe*

Improvising on the 5th and 6th Strings

Below are the notes on the 5th string.

And here are the notes on the 6th string.

Dotted Quarter Notes

Remember that a dot increases a note's value by one half of itself. A quarter note is one beat long. Half the value of 1 is ½. Add these values together and you get one-and-a-half beats (1 + ½ = 1 ½). The *dotted quarter note* lasts for one-and-a-half beats. This is the same value as a quarter note tied to an eighth note.

This solo has a Brazilian feel in the style of João Gilberto and Stan Getz; do not swing the eighth notes. You will have four open choruses to solo over.

Track 70 *Ooh La La*

The Major Scale and Its Use in Improvisation

A *scale* is the arrangement of notes in a particular order. Most popular music is derived from the *major scale*. You may recognize it when sung with the syllables: do–re–mi–fa–sol–la–ti–do.

Remember that a half step is the distance of one fret on the guitar. A *whole step* is the distance of two frets. A major scale consists of whole and half steps in this order:

Whole–Whole–Half–Whole–Whole–Whole–Half

or

W–W–H–W–W–W–H,

or

"Wendy **W**itch **H**as **W**ild, **W**onderful, **W**avy **H**air"

Let's build a C Major scale using the formula above. Start with C, go up a whole step to D, another whole step to E, a half step to F, etc.

W = Whole step
H = Half step

C Major Scale

Track 71

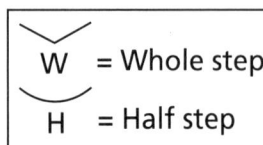

Two important things to remember about the C Major scale:

1. There is always a whole step between the notes:

A–B
C–D
D–E
F–G
G–A

2. There is always a half step between:

B–C
E–F

Let's play a melody that consists entirely of notes from
the C Major scale.

Track 72 · C Major Scale Etude

Swing 8ths

Now improvise your own melodies, using the notes of
the C Major scale in any combination that sounds good
to you. The rhythm section will accompany you for four
choruses.

Track 73 · Song of Major

Swing 8ths

Basic Music Theory

We learned some basic theory in the previous chapter, and we'll continue in this one. Understanding music theory makes it easier to learn an instrument. Theory is the language of music, and it enables musicians to communicate effectively with one another. We will review some of the material that has already been covered in order to build upon it.

The Musical Alphabet

On page 44, you learned that music has a seven-letter, repeating alphabet: A, B, C, D, E, F, G; A, B, C, etc. These are the natural notes; they are neither sharp ♯ nor flat ♭.

Half and Whole Steps

As you know, a half step is the distance of one fret, and a whole step is the distance of two frets. There is either a whole or a half step between one natural note and the next. There is a whole step between: A–B, C–D, D–E, F–G, G–A. There is a half step between: B–C, E–F.

Enharmonic Equivalents

If there is a whole step between two notes, there has to be a note between them. These are referred to as sharps or flats. The note between A and B can be called A-sharp or B-flat. When two pitches have different names but sound the same (played on the same fret), they are enharmonic equivalents (page 61). Here are all 12 notes:

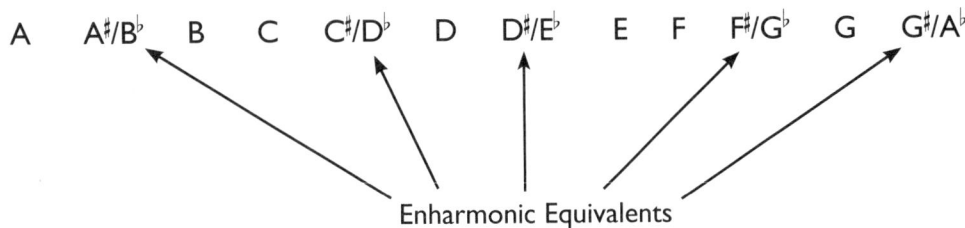

A   A♯/B♭   B   C   C♯/D♭   D   D♯/E♭   E   F   F♯/G♭   G   G♯/A♭

Enharmonic Equivalents

Between each of these notes is the distance of a half step. This half-step movement is called *chromaticism*.

The Musical Alphabet on the Guitar

You can figure out all the notes on the guitar by using the musical alphabet and your knowledge of whole steps and half steps. For example, start with your 1st string. Since that open string is E, the note on the 1st fret (a half step up) is F. The note a half step up from F, on the 2nd fret, is F♯. The note a half step up from this, on the 3rd fret, is G, etc. The illustration to the right gives all the notes on the first four frets of the guitar.

6th 5th 4th 3rd 2nd 1st ← Strings
E   A   D   G   B   E

Frets

F	A♯/B♭	D♯/E♭	G♯/A♭	C	F	1st
F♯/G♭	B	E	A	C♯/D♭	F♯/G♭	2nd
G	C	F	A♯/B♭	D	G	3rd
G♯/A♭	C♯/D♭	F♯/G♭	B	D♯/E♭	G♯/A♭	4th

More on the Major Scale

The major scale consists of seven different notes, eight if you include the *octave* (the distance of 12 half steps between two notes of the same name). As you remember from page 70, the order of whole and half steps is the same for every major scale: Whole–Whole–Half–Whole–Whole–Whole–Half.

What distinguishes major scales from each other is the note that it starts on; this note, from which the scale receives its name, is called the *tonic*. So if you begin the step pattern mentioned above on A, you will have an A Major scale, and the notes will be different than when you start on C.

Following is a C Major scale. Notice that the notes in the scale are numbered: 1, 2, 3, 4, 5, 6, 7, 8. These numbers indicate *scale degrees*. The first note is 1, the second note is 2, etc. The half steps fall between 3 and 4 and between 7 and 8.

C Major Scale

Now, let's start on G and follow the order of whole steps and half steps to make a G Major scale. A whole step up from G is A, another whole step up is B, a half step up is C, a whole step up is D, a whole step up is E, a whole step up is F♯ (because there is only a half step between E and F, we need to sharp the F to make it a whole step), and a half step up brings you back to G.

G Major Scale

How Chords Are Built

The chords you've learned in this book are derived from the major scale. Remember, a chord is three or more notes played simultaneously. The most basic kind of chord is a *triad* (three-note chord). All *major chords* (chords with single-letter names, like the C chord) and minor chords are triads.

To build a triad, use every other note in the major scale. For example, to find the notes in a C chord, simply take the 1(C), 3(E), and 5(G) from the C Major scale. Note that a chord receives its name from the first note, or *root*, upon which it is built.

C Major Scale   C Chord

```
1       3       5                                  Root
C       E       G
```

You might be thinking, "but the C chord I know has four notes, not three," and you'd be correct, but let's take a closer look at these notes. The lowest note in the C chord that you learned on page 19 is E (4th string, 2nd fret)*; then comes G, C, and E once again. All we did was *double*

(repeat) the E by playing it in another octave. Though we played four strings, there are still only three different notes in this chord: E, G, and C. Keep in mind that the notes of a chord may be played in any order and any note within a chord may be doubled or even tripled.

C Major Scale (two octaves)   C Chord

```
        3       5       8(1)    3                  Doubled note
        E       G       C       E
```

In this way, you can build a chord on any note of the scale. Let's build a triad on the 5(G). From G, skip a scale degree to 7(B), then skip another scale degree (past 8

where the scale starts over again) to 2(D). The notes of a G chord are: G, B, D.

C Major Scale   G Chord

```
        5       7       2
        G       B       D
```

The chords built on the 1, 4, and 5 are major; those built on the 2, 3, and 6 are minor. The chord built on 7 is a *diminished* chord and is indicated by the abbreviation "dim" or the symbol ∘ (see top of next page). Roman numerals are used to label the chords built from a particular scale.

Roman Numeral Review		
Upper Case	Lower Case	Arabic
I	i	1
II	ii	2
III	iii	3
IV	iv	4
V	v	5
VI	vi	6
VII	vii	7

* There are many ways to play any chord of a given name.

Notice that major chords are written in upper case Roman numerals; minor and diminished chords are in lower case. The chord built on the first degree of the scale is the *I*, the chord built on the second scale degree is *ii*, etc. Here are all the triads that can be derived from the C Major scale.

Keys

The pattern above—of major, minor, and diminished chords—is the same for every major scale. Different major scales and the chords that come from them are called *keys*. For example, if the melody and chords of a song come from the C Major scale, it is said to be "in the key of C."

I, IV, V—The Primary Chords

The *I, IV,* and *V*—the *primary chords*—are the most commonly used chords in a given key. For an illustration of this, take a look at "12-Bar Blues in A" (which is in the *key of A*) on page 22. It has three chords: A, D, and E. Using whole steps and half steps to find the notes in the A Major scale we get: A–B–C#–D–E–F#–G#–A. Remember that in any key, the I, IV, and V chords are major. As you can see below, the primary chords in the key of A are A, D, and E.

To find the chords for a 12-bar blues progression in any key, figure out the notes in the major scale, then build the chords on the 1, 4, and 5. These chords—the I, IV, and V—are usually played in this order:

More Power Chords

We know that power chords are absolutely essential to rock guitarists. Now, we're going to learn a *chord shape* (moveable chord form) that will allow you to play power chords up and down the neck, starting on any note.

Root-6 Power Chords

Remember, the note that gives a chord its name is called the root. For example, the root of a G chord is the note "G"; because its root is on the 6th string, it is a *root-6* chord. Usually, the root is the lowest note in a chord, but this is not always the case (as we learned with the C chord on page 74).

The G5 Chord

Put your 1st finger on the 3rd fret of the 6th string. Put your 3rd or 4th finger (whichever is more comfortable) on the 5th fret of the 5th string. Strike only the 6th and 5th strings.

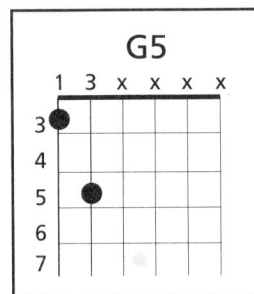

This shape is extremely useful; just move it up or down the neck to play other root-6 power chords. The note that your 1st finger is on, the root, gives each chord its name; your 3rd (or 4th) finger is always two frets up on the 5th string. By referring to the chart for Notes on the 5th and 6th Strings (page 78), you can find all of the different root-6 power chords.

The F5 Chord

To play F5, find "F" on the 6th string; it is on the 1st fret. So, put your 1st finger on the 1st fret of the 6th string. Now put your 3rd (or 4th) finger, two frets up, on the 3rd fret of the 5th string. Strike the 6th and 5th strings only.

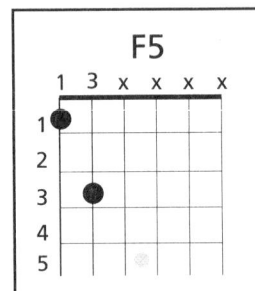

The A5 Chord

To play A5, find "A" on the 6th string; it is on the 5th fret. Put your 1st finger on the 5th fret of the 6th string. Now put your 3rd (or 4th) finger, two frets up, on the 7th fret of the 5th string. Strike the 6th and 5th strings only.

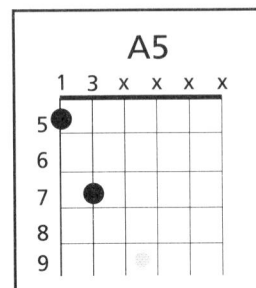

Here's a riff that uses E5, G5, and A5.

Simple Riff

```
        E5      G5      A5      G5      E5
4/4     ■       ■       ■       ■       ◇

Count:  1       2       3       4       1   2   3   4

T
A
B   2       5       7       5       2
    0       3       5       3       0
    2       3       3       3       2
    0       1       1       1       0
```

Root-5 Power Chords

These have the same shape as the root-6 power chords, but your 1st finger is on the 5th string, where the root is, and your 3rd (or 4th) finger is two frets up on the 4th string. You can find any root-5 power chord by referring to the chart for Notes on the 5th and 6th Strings (page 78).

The B5 Chord

To play B5, find "B" on the 5th string; it is on the 2nd fret. Put your 1st finger on the 2nd fret of the 5th string. Now put your 3rd (or 4th) finger on the 4th fret of the 4th string. Strike the 5th and 4th strings only.

```
        B5
    x 1 3 x x x
2   ●
3
4       ●
5
6
```

The C5 Chord

To play C5, find "C" on the 5th string; it is on the 3rd fret. Put your 1st finger on the 3rd fret of the 5th string. Now put your 3rd (or 4th) finger on the 5th fret of the 4th string. Strike the 5th and 4th strings only.

```
        C5
    x 1 3 x x x
3   ●
4
5       ●
6
7
```

```
◇ = Half strum
    gets two beats
```

Swamp Thing

```
        A5      C5      B5          A5      C5      B5      G5      A5
4/4     /       /       ◇           /       /       /       /       ◇

Count:1         2       3       4       etc.

T
A
B   2       5       4       2       5       4           2
    0       3       2       0       3       2           0
    2       3       3       2       3       3       3   2
    0       1       1       0       1       1       1   0
```

Notes on the 5th and 6th Strings

String																									
E	F	F#/Gb	G	G#/Ab	A	A#/Bb	B	C	C#/Db	D	D#/Eb	E	F	F#/Gb	G	G#/Ab	A	A#/Bb	B	C	C#/Db	D	D#/Eb	E
B	C	C#/Db	D	D#/Eb	E	F	F#/Gb	G	G#/Ab	A	A#/Bb	B	C	C#/Db	D	D#/Eb	E	F	F#/Gb	G	G#/Ab	A	A#/Bb	B
G	G#/Ab	A	A#/Bb	B	C	C#/Db	D	D#/Eb	E	F	F#/Gb	G	G#/Ab	A	A#/Bb	B	C	C#/Db	D	D#/Eb	E	F	F#/Gb	G
D	D#/Eb	E	F	F#/Gb	G	G#/Ab	A	A#/Bb	B	C	C#/Db	D	D#/Eb	E	F	F#/Gb	G	G#/Ab	A	A#/Bb	B	C	C#/Db	D
5th string → A	A#/Bb	B	C	C#/Db	D	D#/Eb	E	F	F#/Gb	G	G#/Ab	A	A#/Bb	B	C	C#/Db	D	D#/Eb	E	F	F#/Gb	G	G#/Ab	A
6th string → E	F	F#/Gb	G	G#/Ab	A	A#/Bb	B	C	C#/Db	D	D#/Eb	E	F	F#/Gb	G	G#/Ab	A	A#/Bb	B	C	C#/Db	D	D#/Eb	E

Frets: 3   5   7   9   12   15   17   19   21   24

Below is a song that consists entirely of power chords. It's in the style of "Satisfaction" by The Rolling Stones. Using the chart above, experiment by playing both root-5 and root-6 forms of the chords. Decide for yourself what sounds best.

Track 77 *Dissatisfied*

E5 .... A5 ....

E5 .... A5 ....

E5 ...... B5 ...... E5 ...... A5 ......

E5 ....

Basic Lead Guitar

Soloing is an important part of blues guitar, especially electric blues. Usually, blues players improvise their solos, spontaneously creating melodies as they go along. This requires some basic techniques and a vocabulary of musical ideas. The point of this chapter is to help you understand how this works and to get you started.

B
L
U
E
S

Note

A solo is usually *accompanied,* or backed up, by musicians known as the *rhythm section;* in the blues, this usually consists of a drummer, bass guitarist, and rhythm guitarist. The melodies in this chapter are in the key of A, so they sound good when accompanied by the chords of a 12-bar blues in A.

The Minor Pentatonic Scale

The *minor pentatonic scale* is the most frequently used scale in blues improvisation. It has five notes ("penta" is the Greek word for five) instead of the seven notes of the major scale, so it's much easier to remember and use.

The A Minor Pentatonic Scale

Notice that, even though the scale has five notes (A–C–D–E–G), it can be repeated in different octaves.

The next step is to create melodies from the notes of the minor pentatonic scale. Here are a few guidelines to help you get started. Remember that they are just that, guidelines, not rules. Use your ears. The only real rule is: If something sounds good, it is good.

1. Play Notes that Are Close to Each Other

When just learning to improvise, it sounds better if you play notes that are near each other in the scale; it's also easier. Later, you can experiment by playing notes that are farther apart. Below is a short melodic idea. When you can play it, try making your own, using similar notes and ideas.

Example 1

Track 79 *Swing 8ths*

```
        A5              D5                 A5
T--1---------1----3--1--3----0----1-------------------
A------2------------------------------2-----2---------
B----------------------------------------------------
     1   2   1    3  1  3  0  1     2     2
```

2. Play Short Phrases

A *phrase* is a musical idea. *Phrasing* is the art of stringing these ideas together. Think of taking a solo as being like speaking: You'll get your point across better if you take pauses and speak in clear, concise sentences. Following are two short phrases separated by pauses, which give emphasis to the separate musical ideas.

Example 2

Swing 8ths

Track 80

```
        A5              D5              A5
T--0--0-------------0----------------------------1------
A----------------------3--1---3---1-----2---------------
B------------------------------------------------------
     0  0          0  3  1   3   1    2           1
```

3. End Phrases on the Tonic

Remember, the tonic is the first note in the scale, the one that gives the scale its name. This is definitely not a rule, but when you're starting to improvise, it's easier to make a phrase sound like it has an ending if you end it on the tonic. Try playing around with the minor pentatonic scale, ending phrases on the tonic. Refer to Example 1 on this page for an illustration of this point.

Below is a solo over a 12-bar blues in A. When you can play it, try making up your own, then writing it down and practicing it. This process will start you on your way as an improviser and will sharpen your soloing skills. Remember, it's okay to repeat yourself: When you speak, words and phrases are often repeated either to emphasize points or create new meaning in a different context.

Track 81 — A Minor Pentatonic Solo

Track 82 — Here's a backing track for you to jam over.

Comping

Comping means "to accompany." It is what a rhythm guitarist plays to support someone else's solo.

Comping also means "to complement." You are not only providing rhythmic accompaniment but are listening with the intention of making the soloist sound as good as possible.

JAZZ

Here are two techniques to use:

1. Strum with your pick or thumb in a downward motion only. This is the method you have been using so far.

2. *Pluck* the strings with your fingers (see below).

Plucking the Strings with Your Fingers

1. Place the side of your right-hand thumb on the bass string and place your index, middle, and ring fingers on the 3rd, 2nd, and 1st strings.

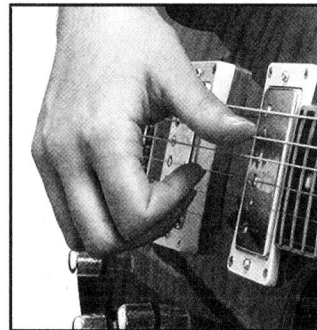

2. Push your thumb down, coming to rest on the string underneath, and simultaneously pluck in toward your palm with all three fingers. Do not pull your hand away from the strings; while the fingers move, the hand and wrist should remain still.

Relax. Don't forget to breathe. Following are some basic comping examples:

Our first pattern is often called "four-on-the-floor" or "Freddie Green" comping (Freddie Green was the guitarist in the Count Basie Orchestra, who used this style his entire career). Be sure to emphasize beats 2 and 4 by counting them louder: **"one—TWO—three—FOUR."** This is called a *backbeat*. Also, it is a nice touch to separate the chord-strums by stopping them with the heel of your hand.

Track 83

CMaj7

Count: 1   2   3   4

You can also vary the rhythms. The following four examples are sparser; think of horns in a big band playing sharp, snappy lines behind a soloist. The big bands of Duke Ellington and Count Basie are great examples of this.

Swing 8ths

CMaj7

Count: 1   &   (2)   &   (3   &   4   &)

Swing 8ths

CMaj7

Count: (1)   &   (2   &)   3   &   (4   &)

Swing 8ths

CMaj7

Count: 1   &   (2   &)   3   &   (4   &)

Swing 8ths

CMaj7

Count: 1   &   (2)   &   (3)   &   (4   &)

You can also try stringing the above examples together, and playing them one after the other. For best results, combine two measures at a time.

Swing 8ths

CMaj7

Count: 1   & (2) &   (3   & 4 &) 1   & (2) &   (3) &   (4 &)

Comping with Dmin, G7, and CMaj7

It's common to comp using the same rhythmic pattern over and over. Let's do this with a chord progression used very frequently in the jazz world.

Comping with CMaj7, Amin7, Dmin, and G7

Now, let's repeat (or "loop") a two-measure rhythmic pattern, using another important progression.

Comping with Dmin and G7

Here is a simpler, but equally important, chord progression. A two-measure rhythmic pattern is used in the first line and is altered in the second.

The E Minor 7 Chord

Here is another chord used frequently in jazz.
The 2nd finger frets the 5th string, 2nd fret.
Strum down over all six strings.

The abbreviation for E minor 7 is Emin7.

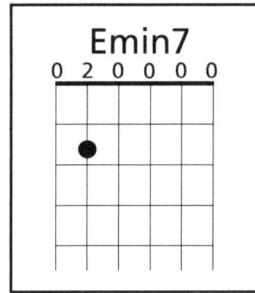

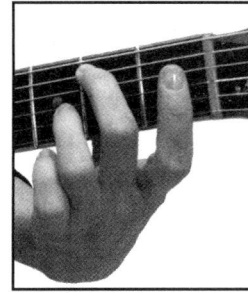

Emin7
0 2 0 0 0 0

Here's a chord progression featuring your new chord.

Track 92 *Turnaround-a-Roo*

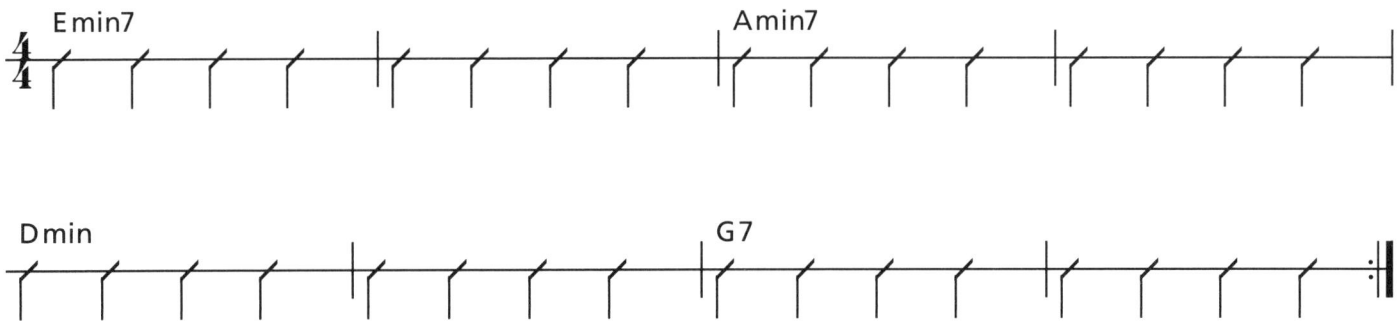

Emin7 · · · · Amin7 · · · ·

Dmin · · · · G7 · · · ·

Let's spice up the progression above with a different comping pattern.

Track 93 *Turnaround-a-Two*

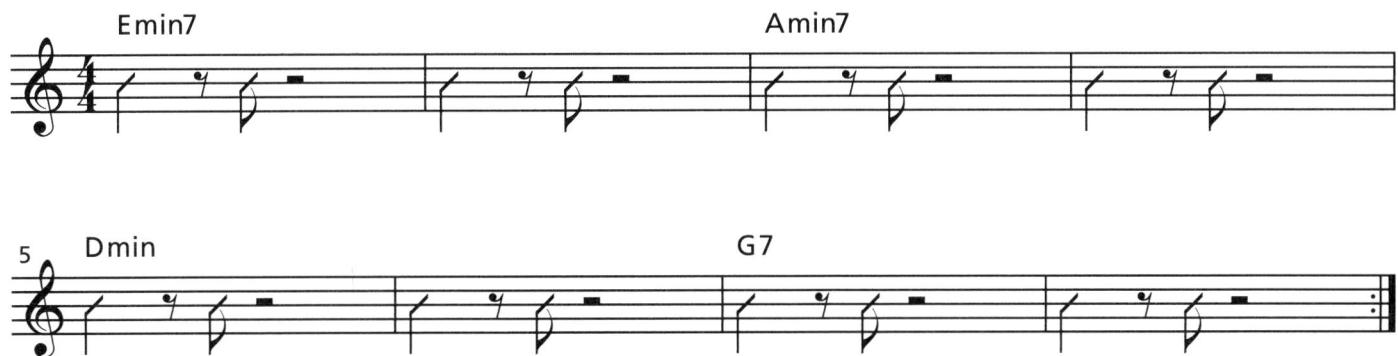

Emin7 · · · · Amin7 · · · ·

Dmin · · · · G7 · · · ·

More Chords and Chord Progressions

On page 74, we talked about how the chords we've been learning come from the major scale. This was demonstrated with the chords C and G, but it also holds true for chords like CMaj7 and Emin7. Remember, to create a chord, all we have to do is start on one note, then pick two or three more notes by skipping every other one.

Example:

Notes of the scale	Notes of the chord	Chord name
C D E F G A B =	C E G B	(These notes make CMaj7)
E F G A B C D =	E G B D	(Emin7)

JAZZ

C Major 7 chord derived from C Major Scale

CMaj7

E Minor 7 chord derived from C Major scale (two octaves)

Emin7

On the next page are a few chord progressions referred to by their Roman numerals. Remember, the number of the chord depends on where the root note falls within the major scale. (If you need a review of this, see pages 74–75.)

The ii–V–I Progression

Two–Five–One (or *ii–V–I*) is another way of saying "Dmin–G7–CMaj7" (when using chords constructed from the notes of the C Major scale). It is the most common chord progression in jazz. Play along with this example.

The I–vi–ii–V Progression

This is another useful progression known as a *turnaround*. A turnaround is a chord, or group of chords, that takes you back to the beginning of a song or progression. It is often repeated several times at the end of a tune as accompaniment for a final solo.

The iii–vi–ii–V Progression

The iii chord can replace the I chord for a slightly different sound.

Soloing Over a 12-Bar Blues—Revisited

Let's take one more spin through a 12-bar blues, improvising with the A Minor Pentatonic scale we learned on page 79. Notice that although the scale has only five notes, we repeat them on higher strings to create more note choices for improvising.

JAZZ

A Minor Pentatonic Scale

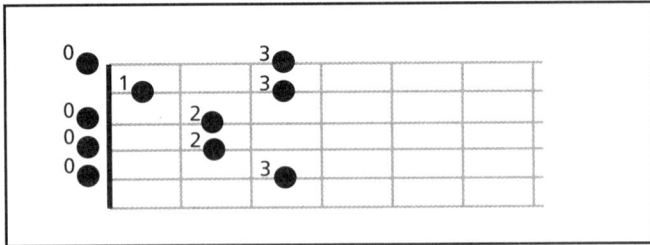

Below is another example of what you can do with this scale. As you know, you can play a solo using a few notes at a time; try this technique with the rhythm section for one open chorus after the example.

Track 97 *A Minor Blues Too*

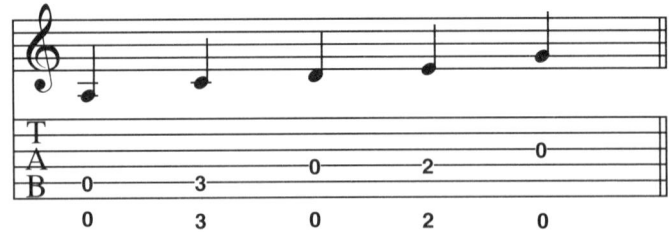

Fingerstyle

Your right hand usually has the job of strumming the guitar. Although the sound is very full, sometimes you need a more delicate sound. An alternative to strumming is *fingerstyle*, or *fingerpicking*. Instead of the notes in a chord being played all at once, they are played individually, or *arpeggiated*. A chord that is played in this manner is called an *arpeggio*.

Each finger on the right hand has a string that it almost always plays.

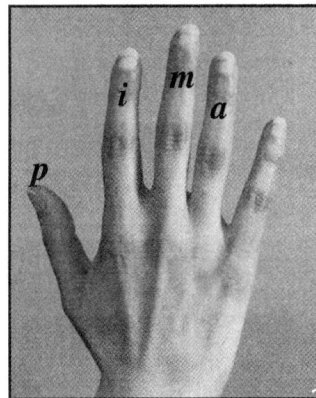

The fingers of the right hand.

> *p* = **Thumb.** Plays the bass strings: 6th, 5th, and 4th.
> *i* = **Index finger.** Plays the 3rd string.
> *m* = **Middle finger.** Plays the 2nd string.
> *a* = **Ring finger.** Plays the 1st string.

To strike the strings with the fingers (*i*, *m*, and *a*), pull them inward towards the palm. The hand should be still and not pull away from the strings. To play the bass notes with *p*, move the whole thumb as one unit across the string towards the *i* finger. Enjoy warming up your fingerstyle technique with "Sunday Picnic" below.

Sunday Picnic

RIGHT-HAND PATTERN

The folk song "Scarborough Fair," made famous by Simon and Garfunkel in the 1960s, is perfectly suited for fingerstyle playing. For this tune, we will use a common picking pattern in $\frac{3}{4}$ time (see right).

This song introduces a new note: the high A on the 5th fret of the 1st string.

1st string
5th fret
4th finger

A

Learn both the melody and the fingerstyle accompaniment for this song. The melody is below, and the accompaniment is on the next page.

Scarborough Fair—Melody

Scarborough Fair—Fingerstyle Accompaniment

Moveable Chords

Some of the most basic chords you know can be moved up the neck (to higher numbered frets), keeping the same fingering. The arrangement of notes will remain exactly the same, but the pitch will move up by a half step each fret. The chord quality (major, minor, etc.) will stay the same. We call this kind of chord a *moveable* chord. Any chord that includes no open strings can be a moveable chord. We just need to know where the root of the chord resides in the fingering, and move the chord up to the new, desired root.

For example, look at the diagrams below. At the 1st fret, we have an F chord. The F chord does not include any open strings. An F chord includes a *barre* across the top two strings. (A barre is when you lay a single finger across two or more strings at the same fret.) The root of the F chord (F) is on the 1st string. If we move it up to the 2nd fret it becomes an F♯ or G♭ chord, because the root at the 2nd fret is a half step higher. At the 3rd fret it becomes a G chord, and so on.

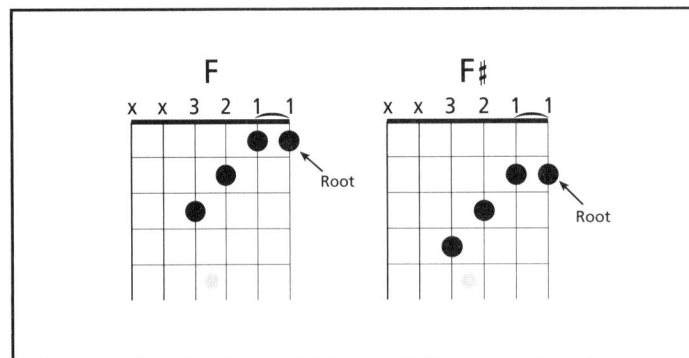

Barre Chords

If a chord does include open strings, it can become a moveable chord by making it a barre chord. To do this, refinger the chord so that the 1st finger is not involved and then move up the neck to the desired fret. As the chord moves up the neck, the 1st finger lays down behind it over the strings, acting like the nut of the guitar.

It takes practice to make barre chords sound clear. They require working all new muscles in your left hand. Make sure that you are holding the guitar in the proper position. If you find that your hand is getting tired or cramped, take a break. You will get a better tone if you barre with the outside, or left side, of your first finger. It is also very helpful to move your left elbow in, closer to your side. Also, be sure never to barre more strings than is necessary for the chord. But the best tip is to practice, practice, practice!

The E-Form Barres

The E chord is one of the most commonly used chords for creating barre chords. Since the 1st finger is needed for the barre, we form the E chord with the other three fingers (2, 3, and 4). The root of this chord is on the 6th string. As the chord moves up the neck, so does the name of the chord. Since the root is on the 6th string, we can call this kind of barre a *root-6 barre*.

The diagram below shows all the notes on the first 12 frets of the 6th string. These are the roots for the root-6 chords.

Root-6 Names for E-Form Barres

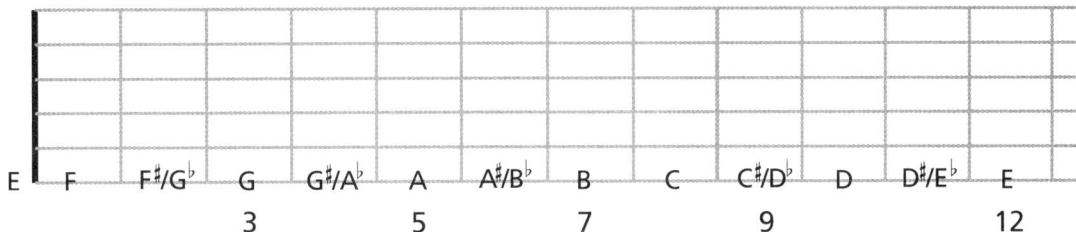

Let's make sure you know the four basic E-form chords: E, E7, Emin, and Emin7. Let's finger them with the 1st finger free to become a barre. Then, let's move them up one fret to become F, F7, Fmin, and Fmin7.

The A-Form Barres

The A chords can be used as barres in the same manner as the E chords. First, however, we have to learn the locations of the A roots. Since, in an A chord, the root is on the 5th string, this type of barre can be called a *root-5 barre*.

The diagram below shows all the notes on the first 12 frets of the 5th string. These are the roots for the root-5 chords.

Root-5 Names for A-Form Barres

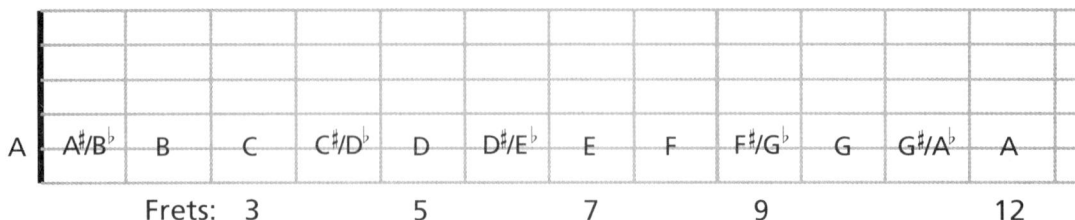

A	A#/B♭	B	C	C#/D♭	D	D#/E♭	E	F	F#/G♭	G	G#/A♭	A

Frets: 3   5   7   9   12

Let's make sure you know the four basic A-form chords: A, A7, Amin, and Amin7. Let's finger them with the 1st finger free to become a barre. Then, let's move them up one fret to become B♭, B♭7, B♭min, and B♭min7. Be patient and have fun!

A
x 0 2 3 4 0

A7
x 0 3 0 4 0

Amin
x 0 3 4 2 0

Amin7
x 0 3 0 2 0

B♭
x 1 2 3 4 1

B♭7
x 1 3 1 4 1

B♭min
x 1 3 4 2 1

B♭min7
x 1 3 1 2 1

"Lessons Learned" uses five barre chords: G, Bmin7, Amin, D7, and C (shown below). Practice switching between them before you try putting them together in the song. Strum down four times in each measure. If there are two chords in the measure, strum twice on each.

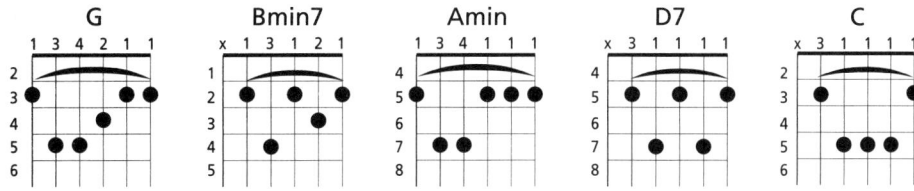

Once you have mastered the chords, enjoy playing the melody, too.

Lessons Learned

Reading Chords

Chord diagrams tell you how to play a particular chord. The fingerings, scale degrees, and position of the chord are all provided on the chord diagram (see below). The photograph to the right shows the finger numbers for the left hand.

When choosing chords, pick those that are close to each other on the neck; this will make for smooth transitions.

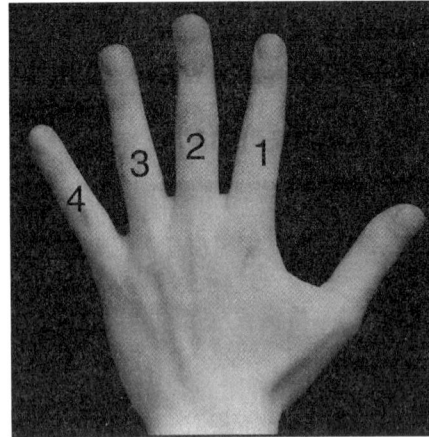

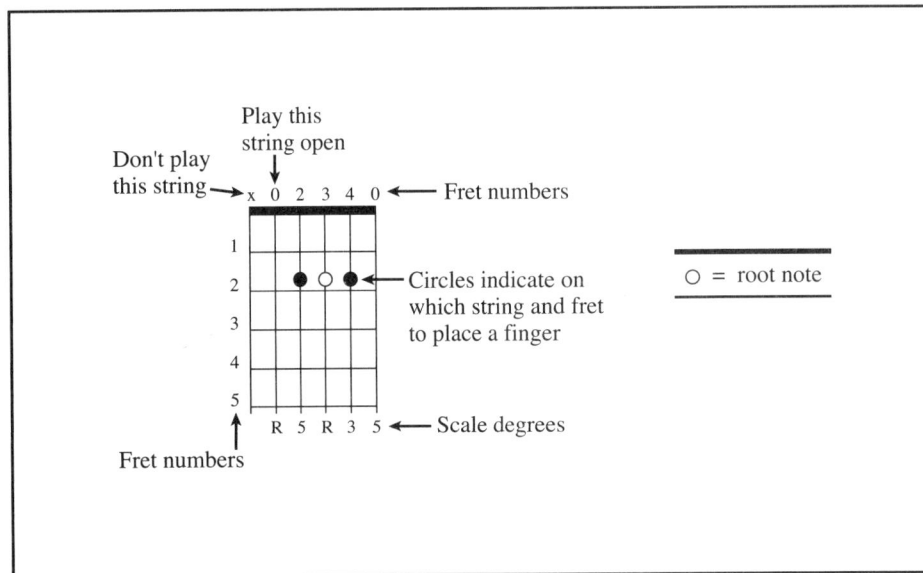

Don't play this string → x

Play this string open

Fret numbers

Circles indicate on which string and fret to place a finger

○ = root note

Fret numbers

R 5 R 3 5 ← Scale degrees

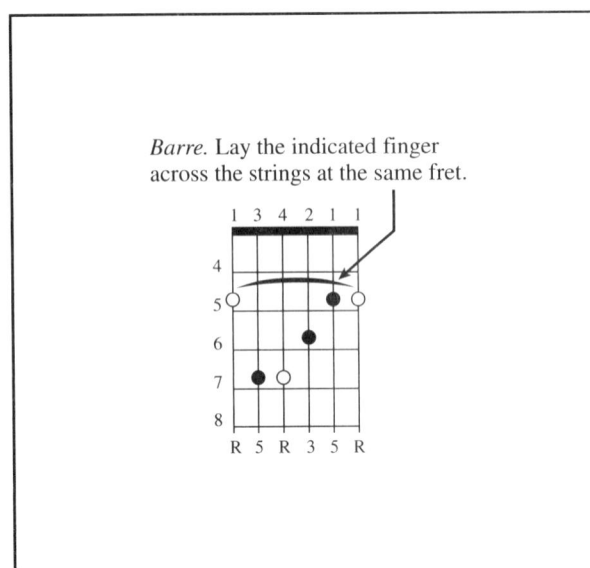

Barre. Lay the indicated finger across the strings at the same fret.

R 5 R 3 5 R

Intervals

An *interval* is the distance in pitch between two notes. You already know two intervals: the whole step and the half step. Now, let's take a closer look.

By counting the note names between two notes, we get a number name. For example, the letter C is three letters away from E. So, the interval from C to E is a *third (3rd)*.

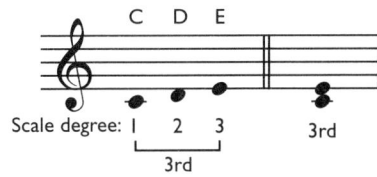

That sounds easy enough, but what would you call a C♯ and E? Or a C and E♭? Their musical distance is different than C and E, so they have to be distinguished from the 3rd in the above example. We solve this problem by *qualifying* the number with the terms *major (M), minor (m), perfect (P)*, and *diminished (d)*.

The examples below illustrate the thirteen intervals—all starting with the C note—within one octave. Play them *harmonically* (together) and *melodically* (in succession) to familiarize yourself with how they sound. Then, play all of them with different starting notes.

Intervals can be described as *consonant* or *dissonant*. A consonant interval is one that sounds stable or resolved—some would say "sweet" or "pleasant." Thirds (3rds) and sixths (6ths) fall into this category. Intervals that are *not* consonant are described as dissonant. They create musical tension and can sound harsh and unresolved. Traditionally, dissonant intervals sound best when they resolve to consonant intervals. The minor 2nd and diminished 5th are examples of dissonance.

Now, let's check out all the intervals.

The Intervals

Chord Theory

It's time to learn more about the different types of chords and how they are made.

Major and Minor Triads

The most basic chords are three-note chords called triads. *Major* and *minor triads* are the most commonly used chords. Keep in mind that the word "major" is only *implied* when talking about major chords. For example, if you are talking about a G Major chord, you would call it a "G" chord. Triads are built by stacking pitches in 3rds.

Let's build a C Major triad. C is the *root* (1) of the chord; E is a 3rd above C, so it is called the 3rd (3) of the chord; G is a 3rd above E and 5th above C, so it is called the 5th (5) of the chord. Like all major triads, it consists of a major 3rd on the bottom and a minor 3rd on the top.

M = Major
m = Minor

You can use the 1, 3, and 5 of any major scale to build a major triad. Lower the 3rd (♭3) of any major triad, or you can think in terms of lowering the 3rd of the scale, and you have a minor triad. Notice that it is a minor 3rd from the 1 to the ♭3 and a major 3rd from the ♭3 to the 5.

Diminished and Augmented Triads

Though they are not used as often as the major and minor, there are two other kinds of triads: *diminished* and *augmented*. A diminished triad consists of two minor 3rds and an augmented triad consists of two major 3rds. In a diminished triad, the 5th is a diminished 5th (or $^\flat 5$), or "d5." In an augmented triad, the 5th is an augmented 5th (or $^\sharp 5$), or "A5."

C Diminished
$1 - {}^\flat 3 - {}^\flat 5$
$C - E^\flat - G^\flat$

C Augumented
$1 - 3 - {}^\sharp 5$
$C - E - G^\sharp$

So, to get a diminished chord (abbreviated as *dim,* or designated with this symbol ○) lower the 5th of a minor triad a half step. To get an augmented chord (abbreviated as *Aug,* or designated with this symbol +), raise the 5th of a major triad a half step.

Chord Voicings

A *voicing* is the way the notes of a chord are stacked or arranged. In common practice, some chord tones are doubled or even tripled in different octaves. This gives us a fuller sound than a three-note voicing.

7 Chords

A "7" chord is built by stacking another 3rd on top of an existing triad. The interval from the root to this added note is a 7th. So the intervals of a 7 chord are 1–3–5–7.

There are many types of 7 chords. We'll look at some of the most common.

Major 7 Chords

A *major* 7 chord (Maj7) is made by placing a major 3rd above a major triad. This additional note is the interval of a major 7th (M7) from the root. The intervals of this chord are 1–3–5–7.

Minor 7 Chords

A *minor* 7 chord (min7) is made by placing a minor 3rd above a minor triad. This additional note is the interval of a minor 7th (m7) from the root. The intervals of this chord are 1–♭3–5–♭7.

Dominant 7 Chords

A *dominant* 7 chord is designated by a "7" (for example, A7, D7, and G7). It is made by placing a minor 3rd above a major triad. This additional note is the interval of a minor 7th from the root. The intervals of this chord are 1–3–5–♭7. The dominant 7th chord is an important part of the blues sound.

The next two types of 7 chords (like the triads they are built on) are not as common as the preceding ones. They can, however, be very effective when used at the right time.

Half Diminished 7 Chords

A *half diminished 7 chord* (min7♭5) is made by placing a major 3rd above a diminished triad. This additional note is the interval of a minor 7th from the root. The intervals of this chord are 1–♭3–♭5–♭7.

Diminished 7 Chords

A *diminished 7 chord* (dim7) is made by placing a minor 3rd above a diminished triad. This additional note is the interval of a diminished 7th (which is a half step lower than a minor 7th) from the root. The intervals of this chord are 1–♭3–♭5–♭♭7. (The symbol ♭♭ indicates a double flat, which tells you to lower the note by two half steps.)

Extended Chords

The term *extended chords* refers to chords that include notes that lie beyond a one-octave major scale. The common tones we add to chords are the 9th, 11th, and 13th.

Extended chords have a lot to do with making jazz sound like jazz. The late, great guitarist Ted Greene was fond of saying that "jazz lives above the 7th." There is much truth to that statement.

Major add 9th Chords

Major add 9th chords are four-note chords. The formula is: R–3–5–9 and the usual chord symbol is add9.

Chord Encyclopedia

Maj
1, 3, 5

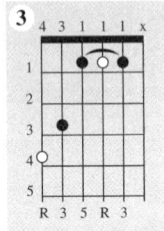 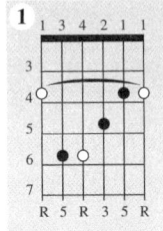 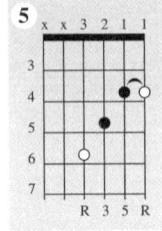 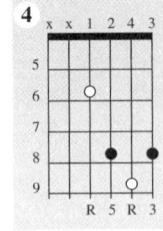 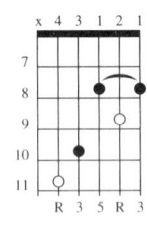 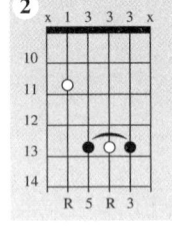

sus2
1, 2, 5

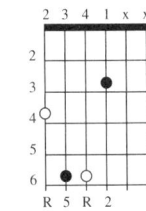 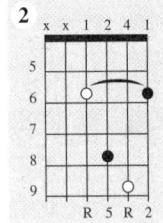 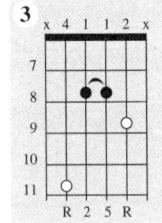 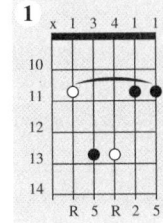 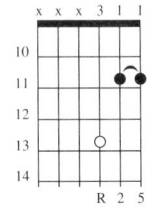

sus4
1, 4, 5

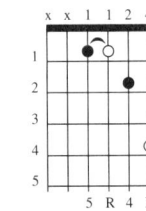 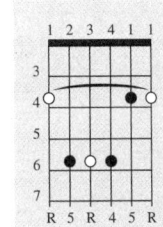 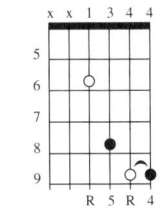 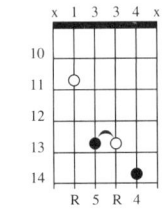

no 3rd
1, 5

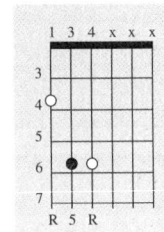 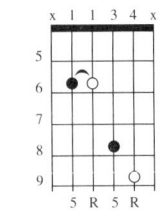 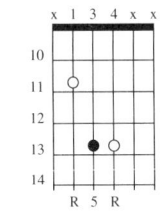

6
1, 3, 5, 6

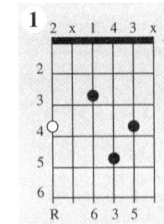 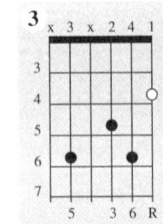 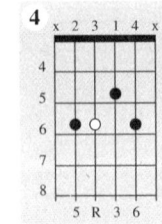  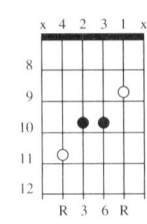 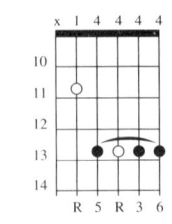

Maj7
1, 3, 5, 7

 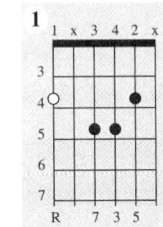 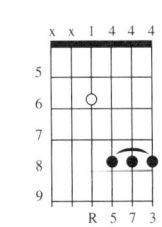 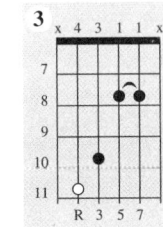 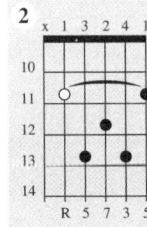 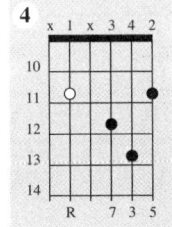

A♭
G♯

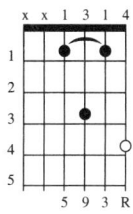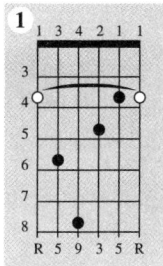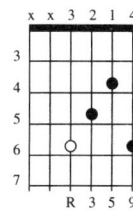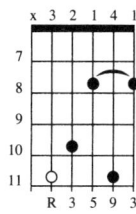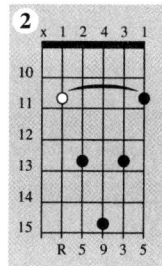

add9
1, 3, 5, 9

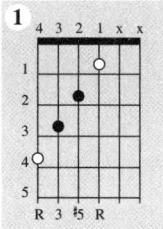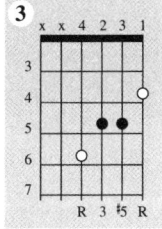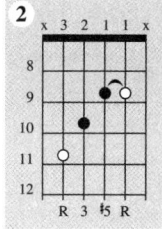

**Augmented
(aug)**
1, 3, ♯5

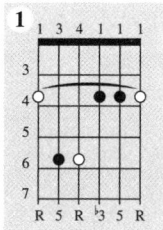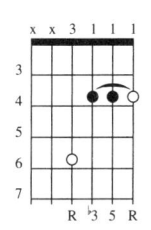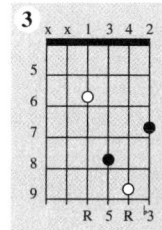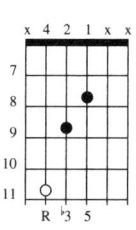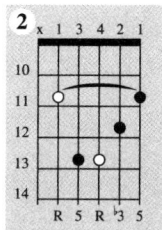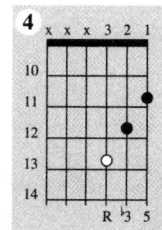

min
1, ♭3, 5

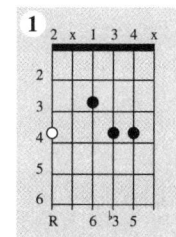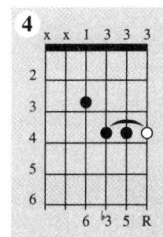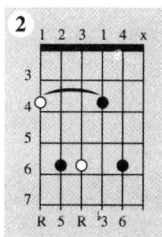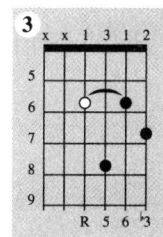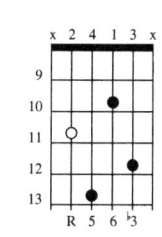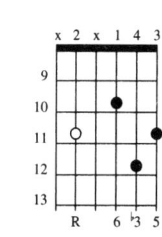

min6
1, ♭3, 5, 6

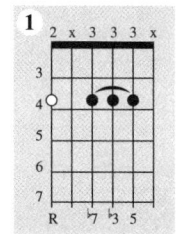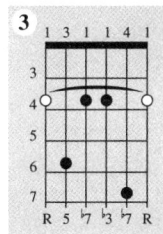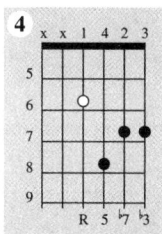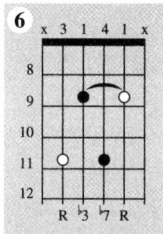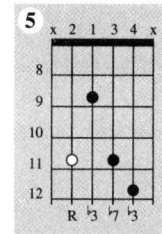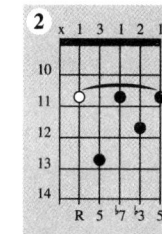

min7
1, ♭3, 5, ♭7

A♭
G♯

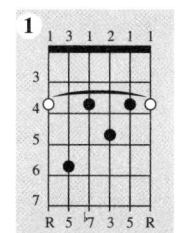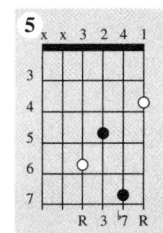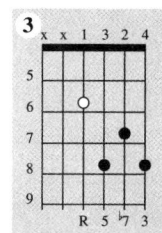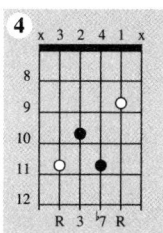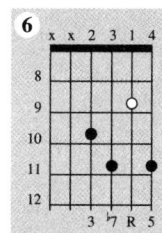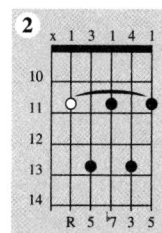

7
1, 3, 5, ♭7

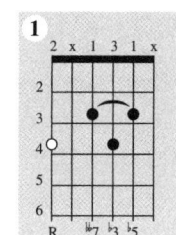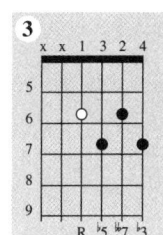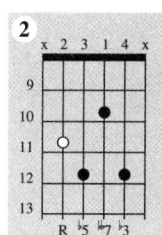

dim7(°7)
1, ♭3, ♭5, ♭♭7

A

Maj
1, 3, 5

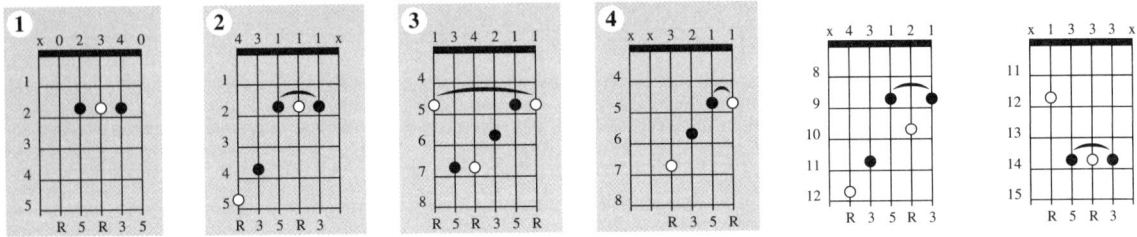

sus2
1, 2, 5

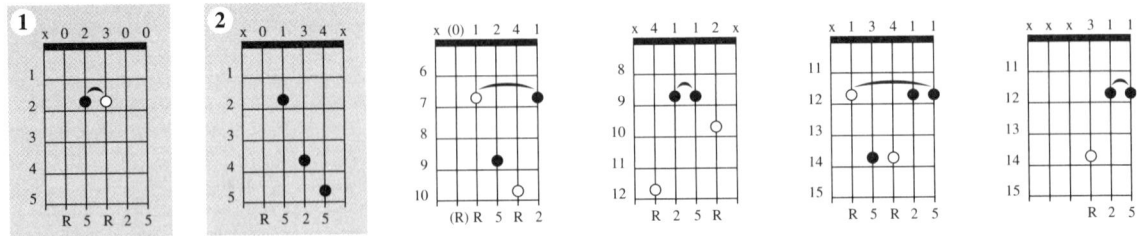

sus4
1, 4, 5

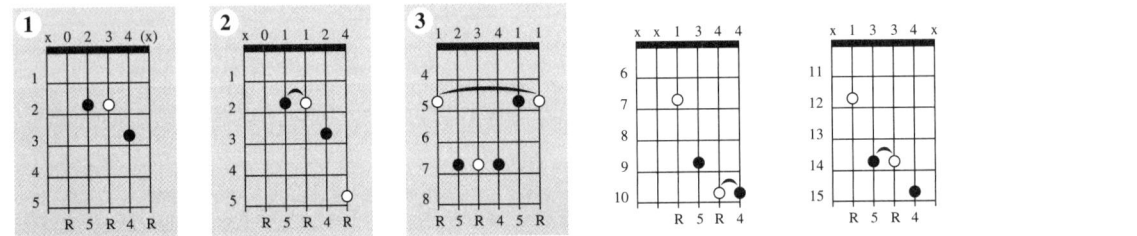

no 3rd
1, 5

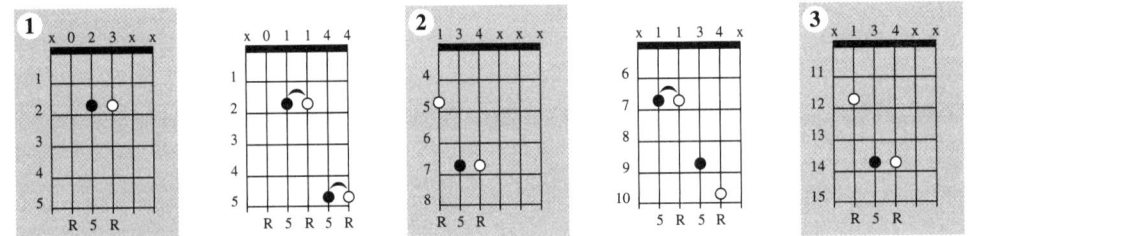

6
1, 3, 5, 6

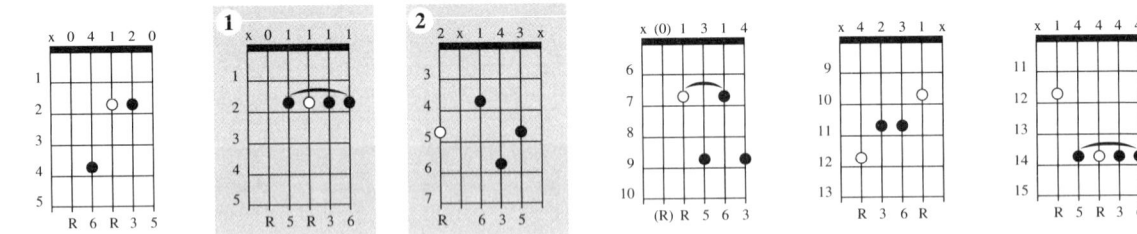

Maj7
1, 3, 5, 7

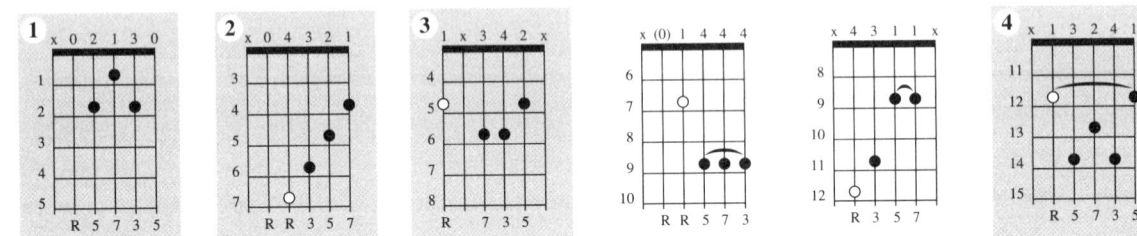

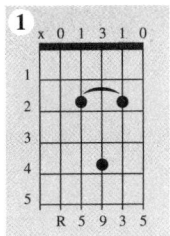 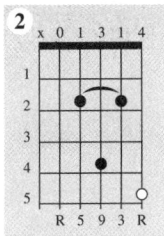 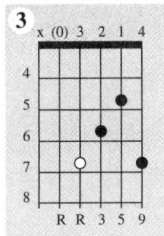 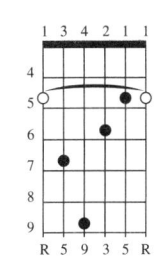 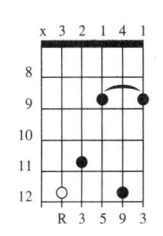 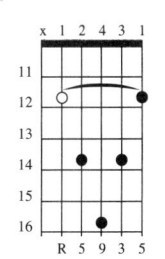

add9
1, 3, 5, 9

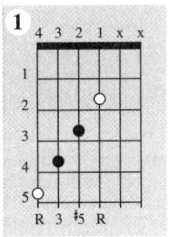 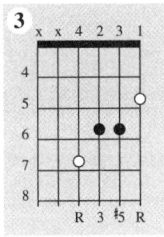 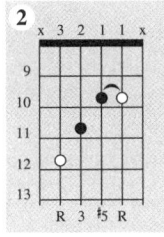

Augmented A
(aug)
1, 3, ♯5

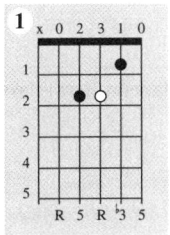 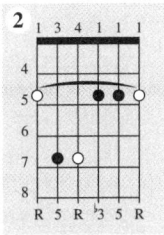 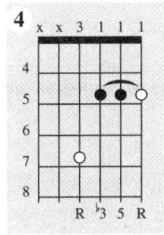 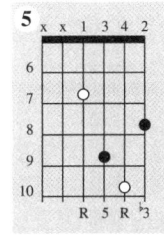 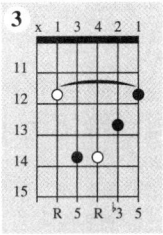 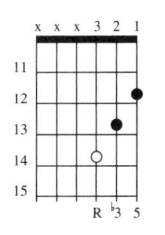

min
1, ♭3, 5

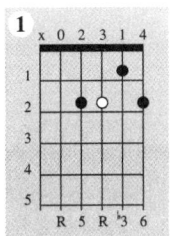 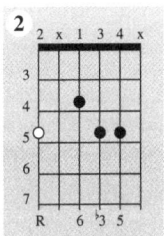 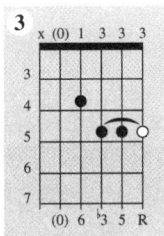 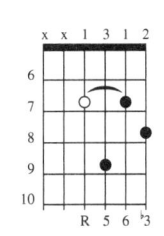 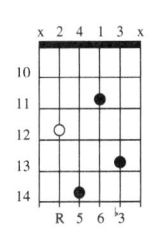 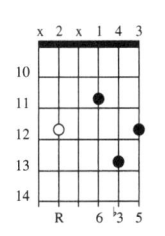

min6
1, ♭3, 5, 6

 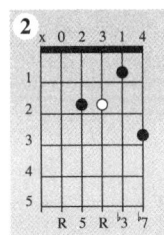 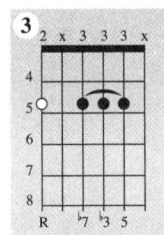 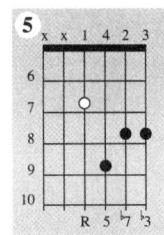 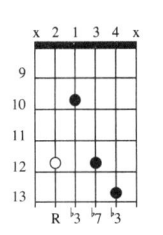 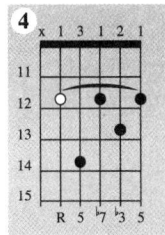

min7
1, ♭3, 5, ♭7

 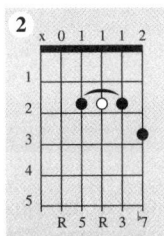 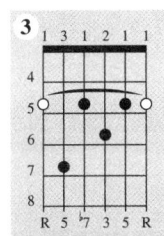 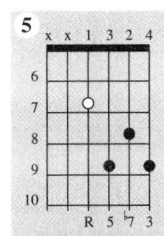 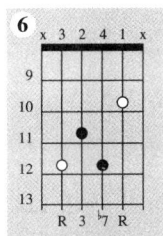 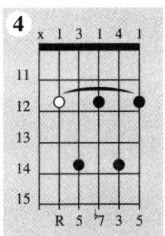

7
1, 3, 5, ♭7

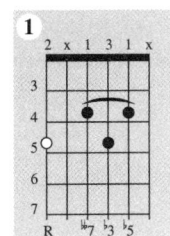 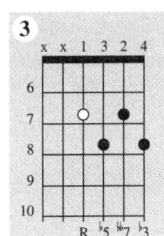 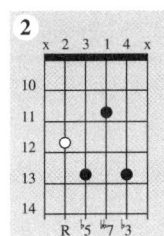

dim7(°7)
1, ♭3, ♭5, ♭♭7

Maj
1, 3, 5

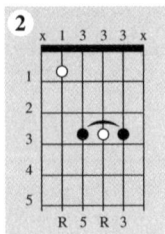 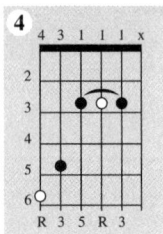 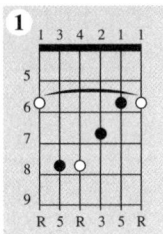 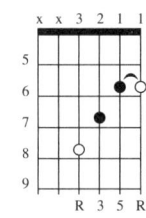 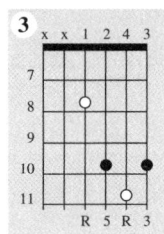 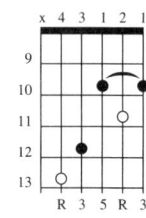

sus2
1, 2, 5

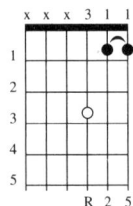 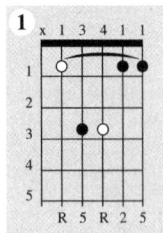 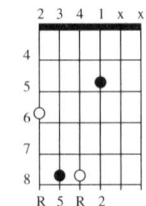 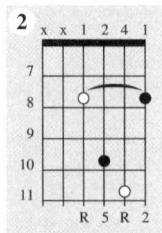 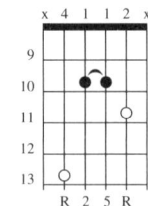

sus4
1, 4, 5

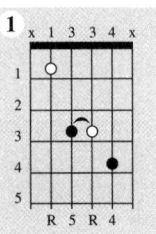 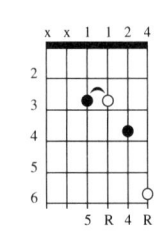 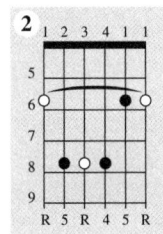 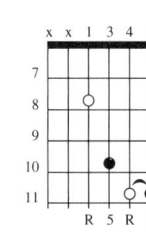

no 3rd
1, 5

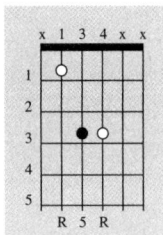 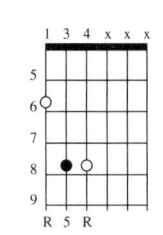 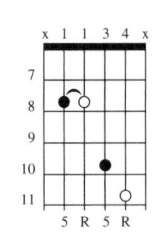

B♭
A♯

6
1, 3, 5, 6

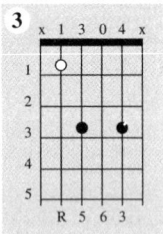 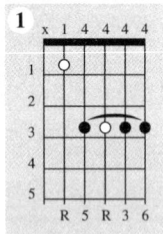 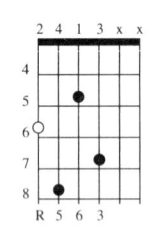 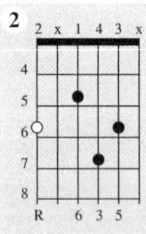 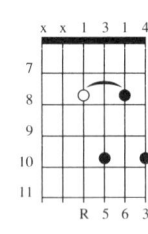 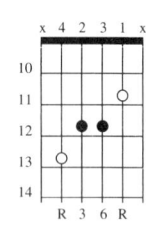

Maj7
1, 3, 5, 7

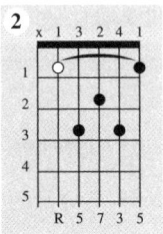 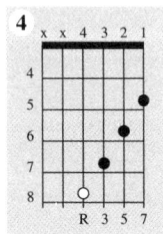 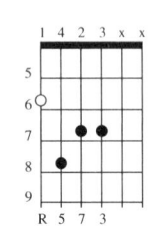 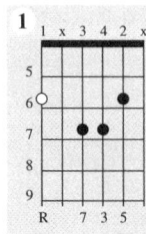 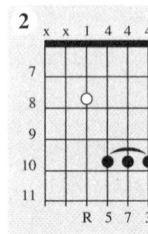 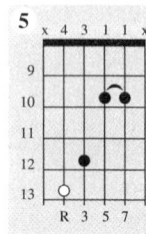

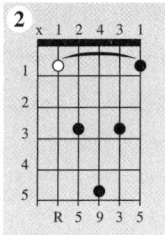 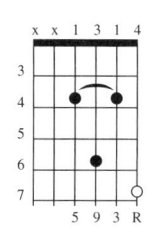 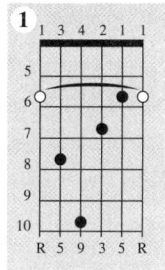 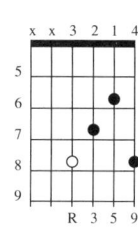 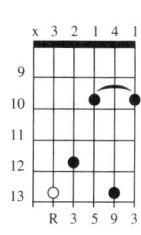

add9
1, 3, 5, 9

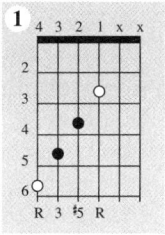 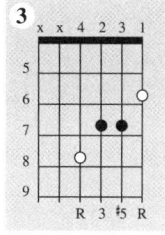 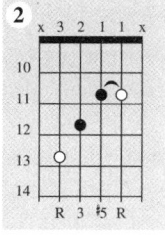

Augmented (aug)
1, 3, ♯5

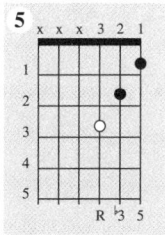 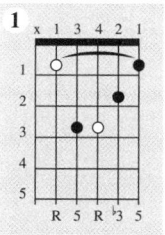 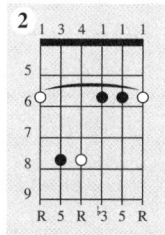 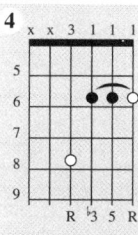 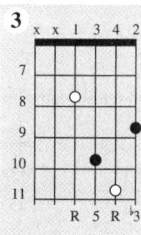 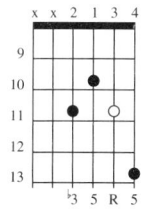

min
1, ♭3, 5

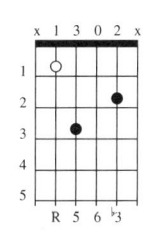 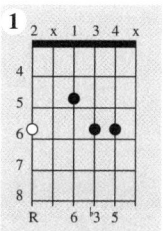 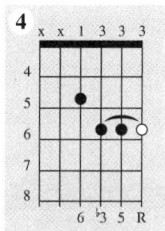 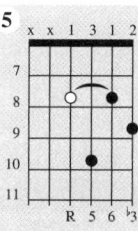 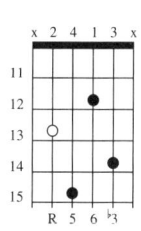 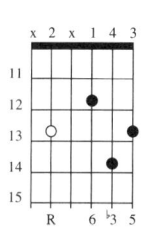

min6
1, ♭3, 5, 6

B♭
A♯

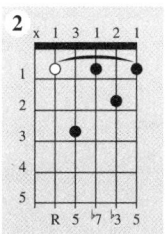 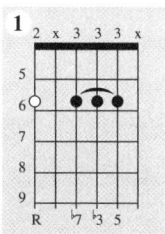 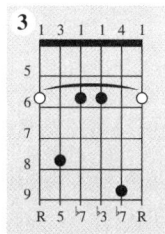 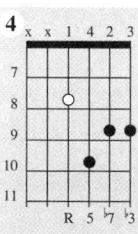 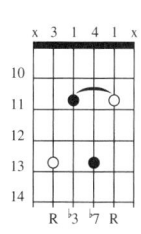 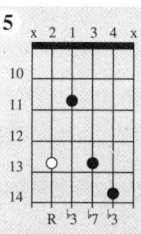

min7
1, ♭3, 5, ♭7

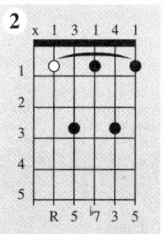 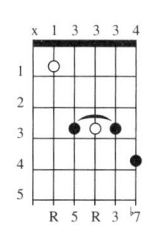 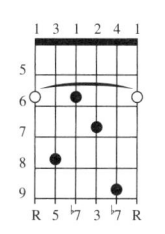 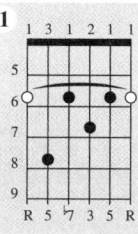 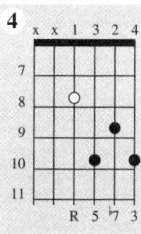 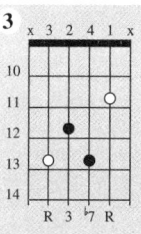

7
1, 3, 5, ♭7

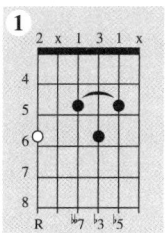 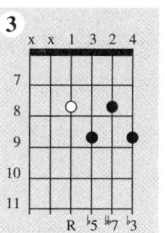 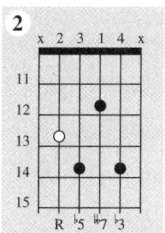

dim7(°7)
1, ♭3, ♭5, ♭♭7

B

Maj
1, 3, 5

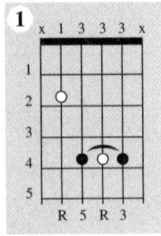 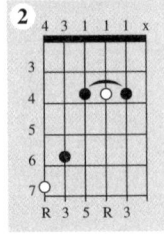 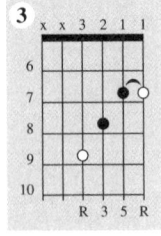 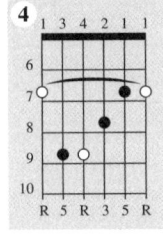 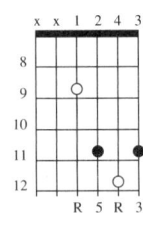 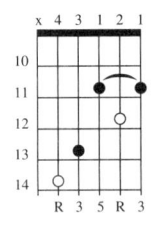

sus2
1, 2, 5

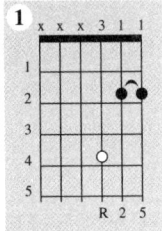 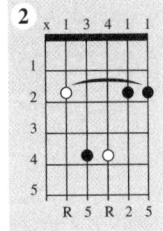 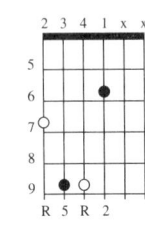 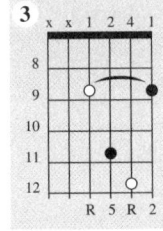 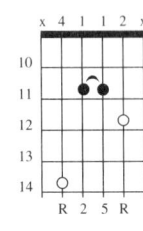

sus4
1, 4, 5

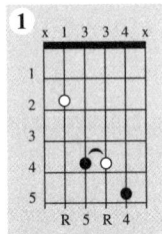 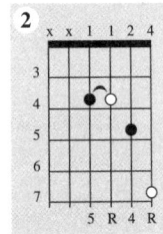 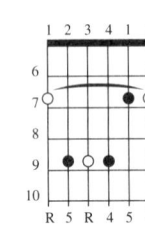 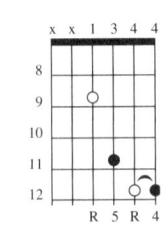

no 3rd
1, 5

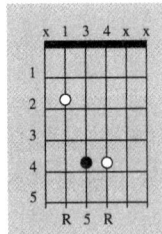 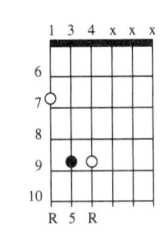 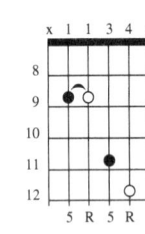

6
1, 3, 5, 6

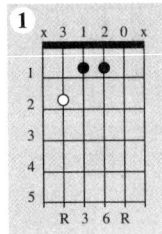 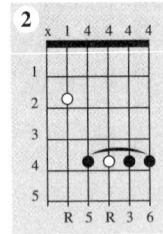 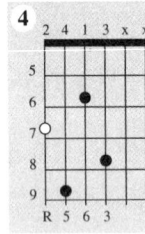 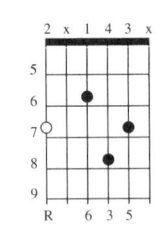 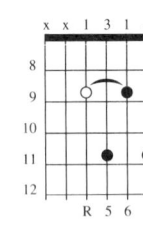 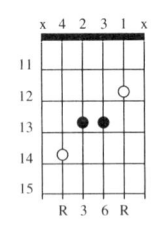

Maj7
1, 3, 5, 7

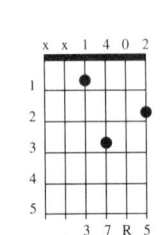   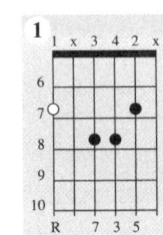 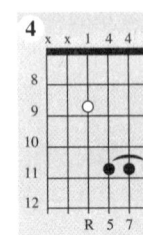 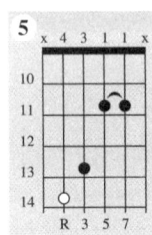

B

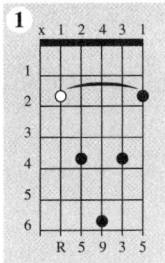 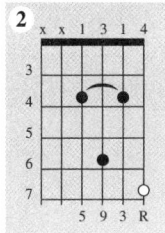 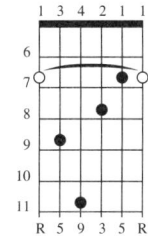 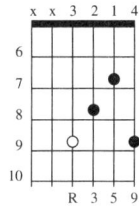 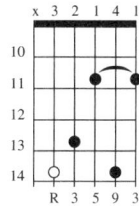

add9
1, 3, 5, 9

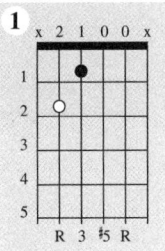 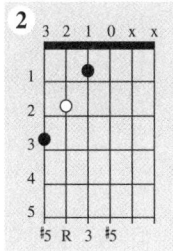 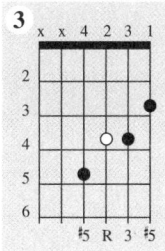 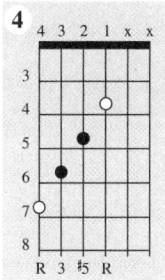 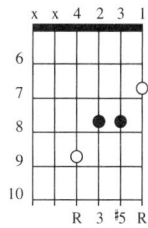

Augmented (aug)
1, 3, ♯5

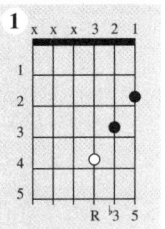 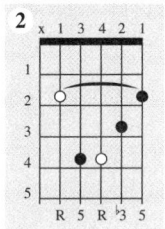 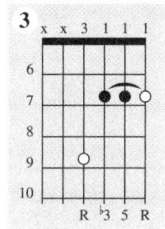 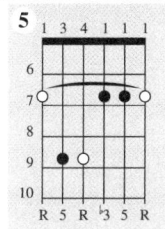 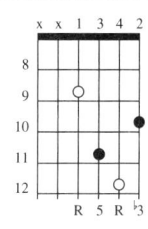 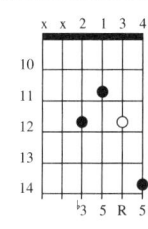

min
1, ♭3, 5

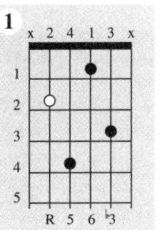 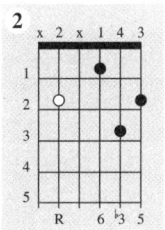 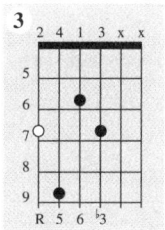 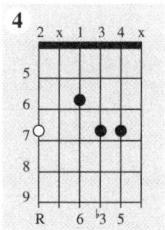 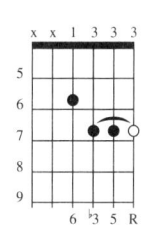 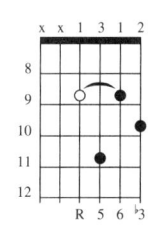

min6
1, ♭3, 5, 6

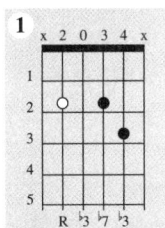 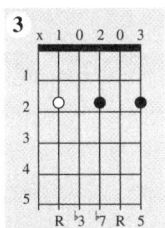 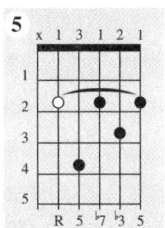 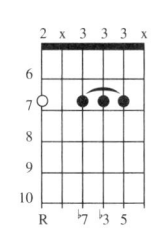 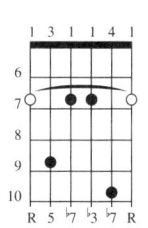 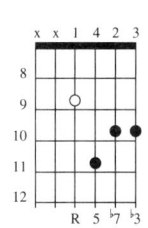

min7
1, ♭3, 5, ♭7

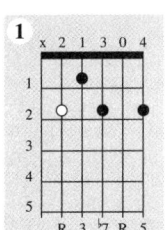 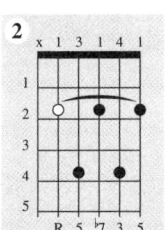 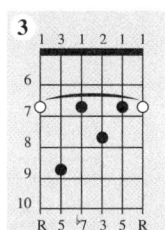 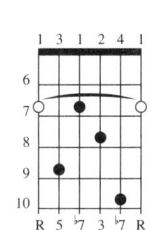 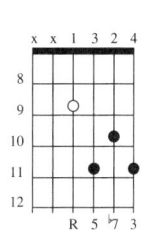 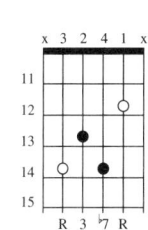

7
1, 3, 5, ♭7

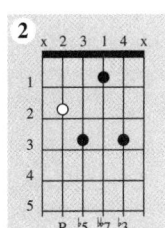 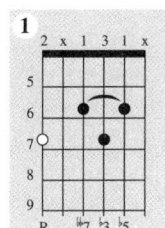 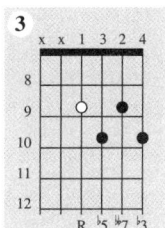

dim7(°7)
1, ♭3, ♭5, ♭♭7

B

Maj
1, 3, 5

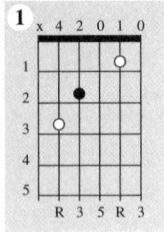 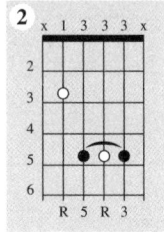 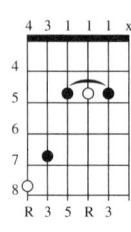 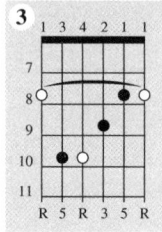 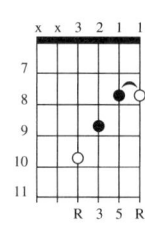 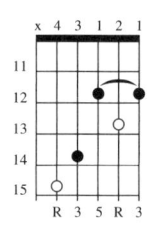

sus2
1, 2, 5

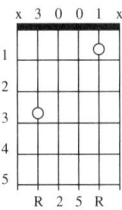 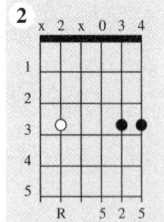 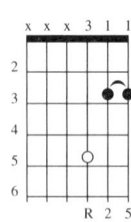 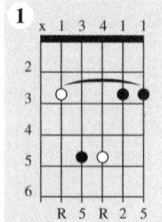 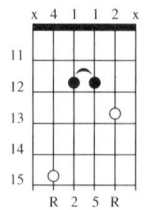 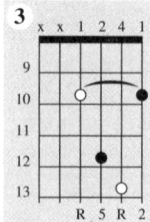

sus4
1, 4, 5

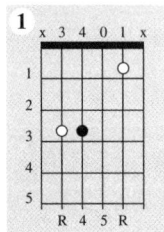 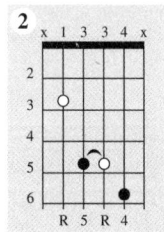 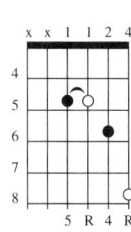 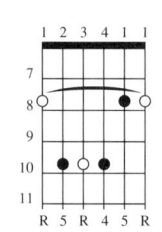 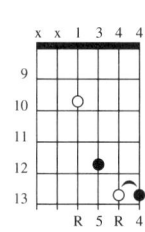

no 3rd
1, 5

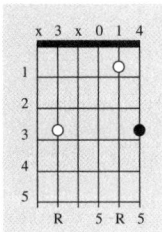 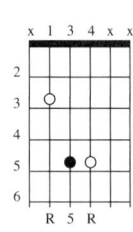 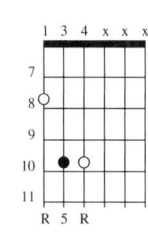 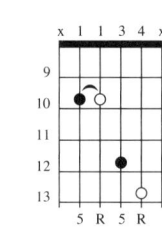

6
1, 3, 5, 6

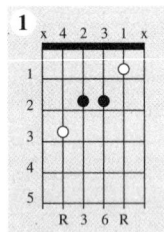 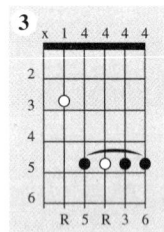 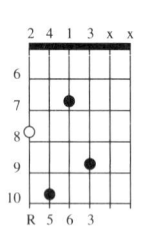 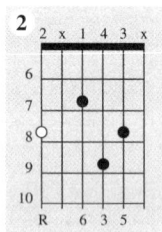 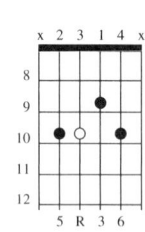 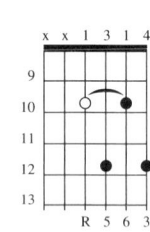

Maj7
1, 3, 5, 7

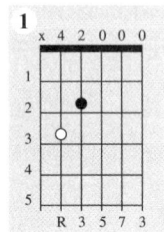  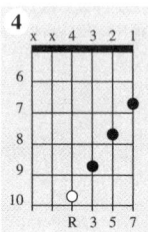 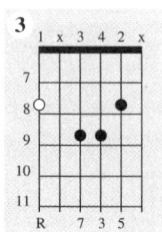 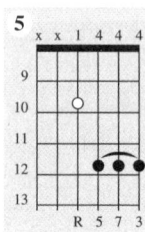 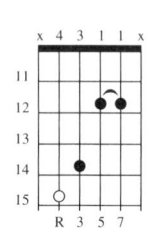

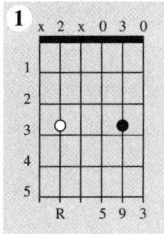 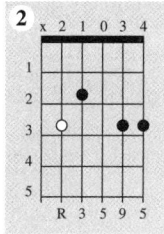 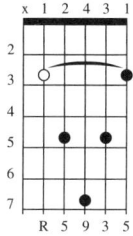 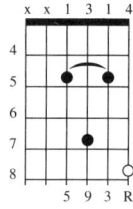 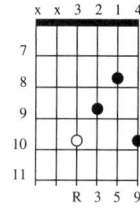 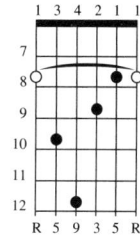

add9
1, 3, 5, 9

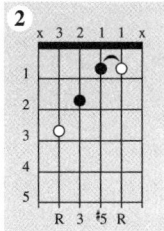 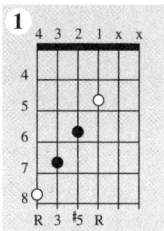 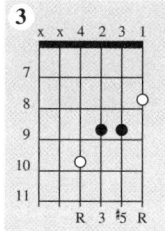

**Augmented
(aug)**
1, 3, ♯5

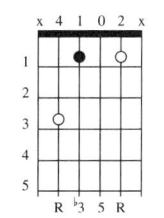 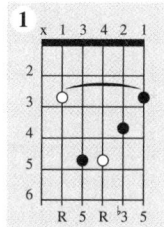 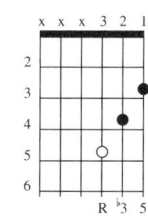 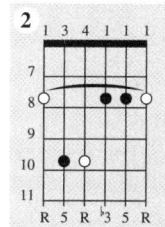 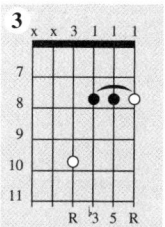 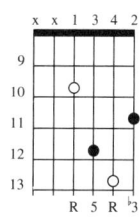

min
1, ♭3, 5

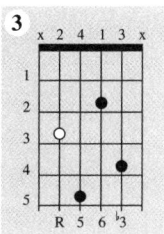 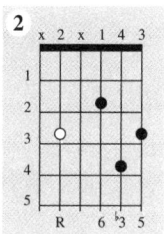 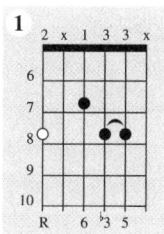 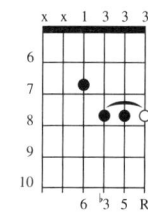 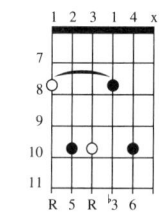 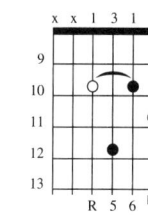

min6
1, ♭3, 5, 6

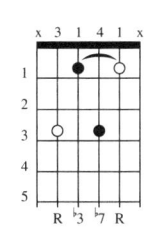 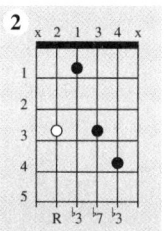 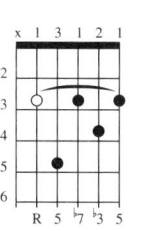 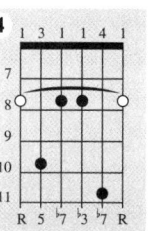 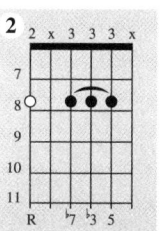

min7
1, ♭3, 5, ♭7

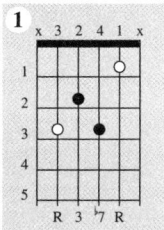 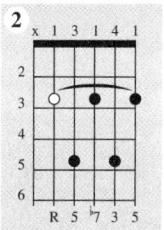 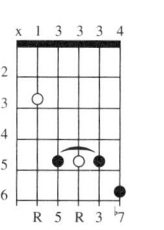 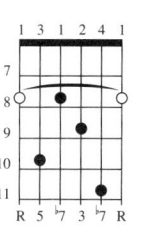 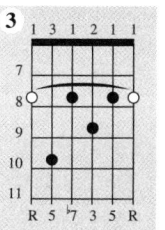 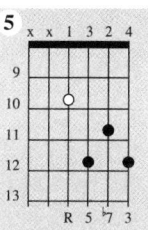

7
1, 3, 5, ♭7

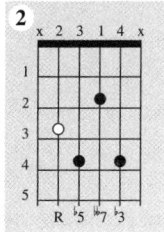 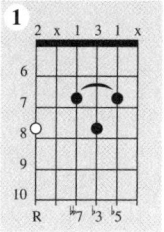 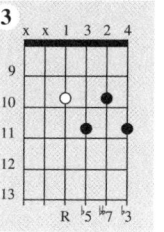

dim7(°7)
1, ♭3, ♭5, ♭♭7

C

Maj
1, 3, 5

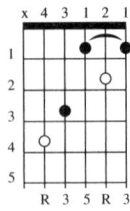 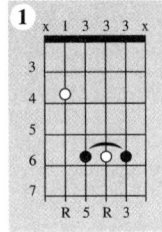 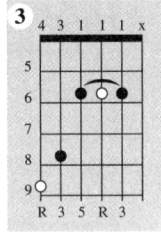 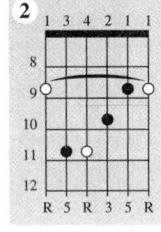 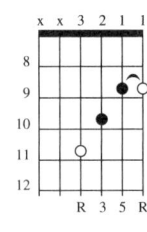 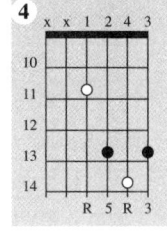

sus2
1, 2, 5

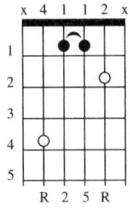 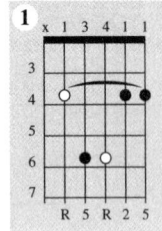 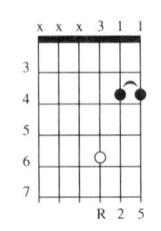 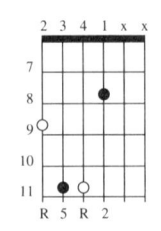 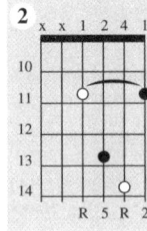

sus4
1, 4, 5

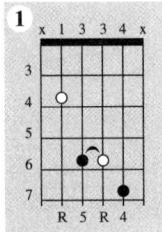 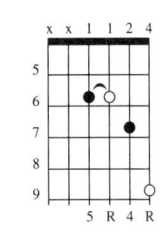 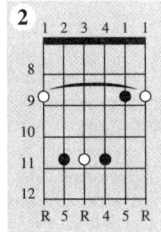 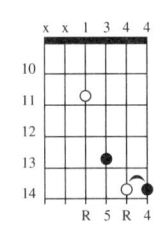

no 3rd
1, 5

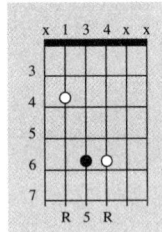 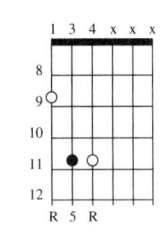 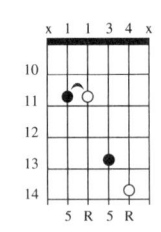

6
1, 3, 5, 6

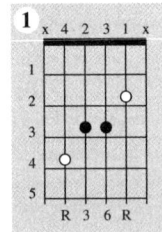 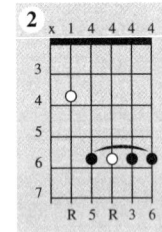 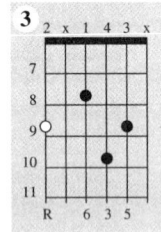 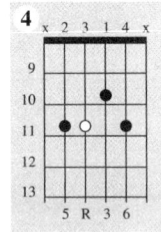 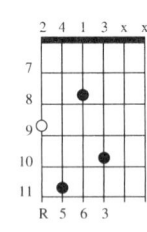 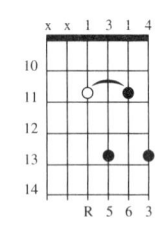

Maj7
1, 3, 5, 7

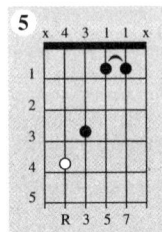 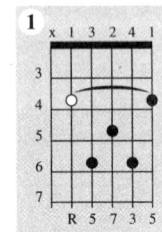  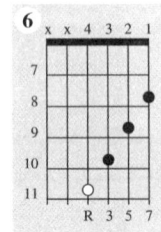 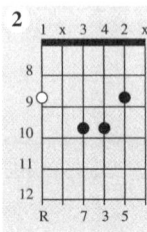 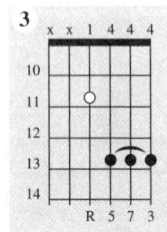

D♭
C♯

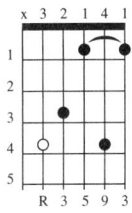 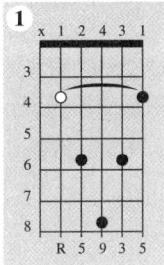 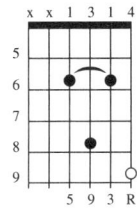 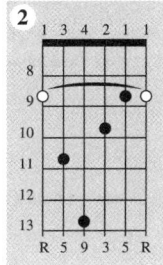 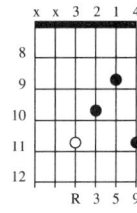

add9
1, 3, 5, 9

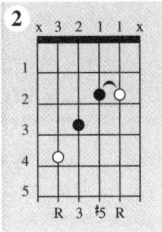 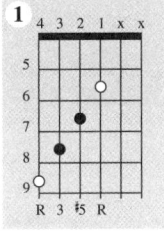 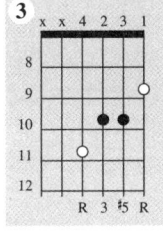

Augmented (aug)
1, 3, ♯5

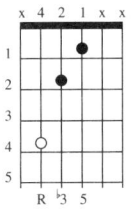 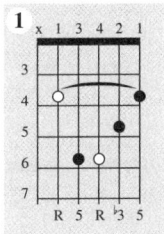 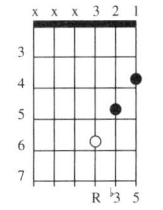 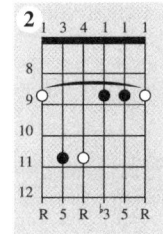 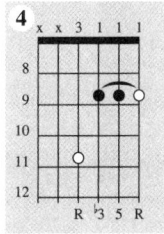 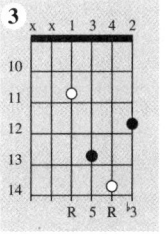

min
1, ♭3, 5

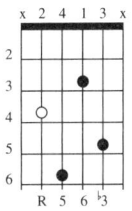 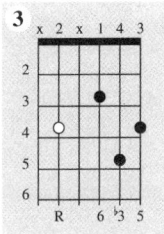 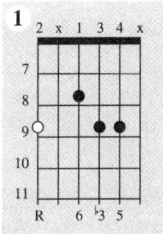 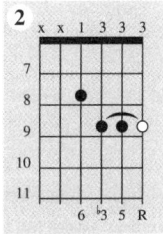 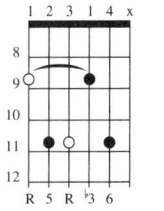 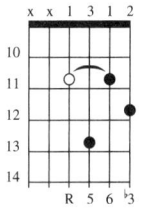

min6
1, ♭3, 5, 6

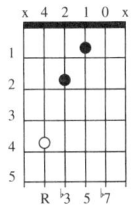 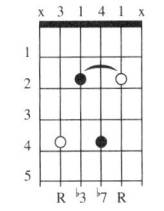 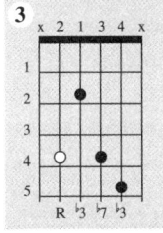 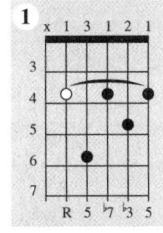 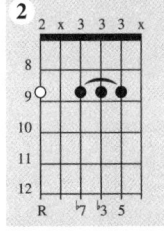 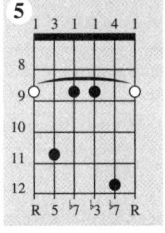

min7
1, ♭3, 5, ♭7

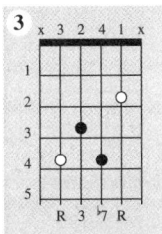 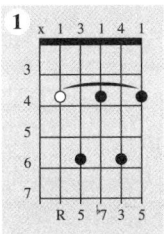 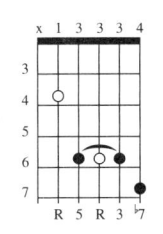 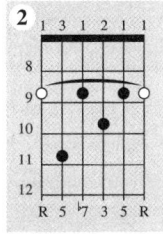 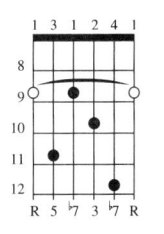 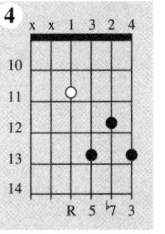

7
1, 3, 5, ♭7

D♭
C♯

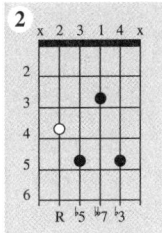 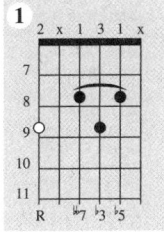 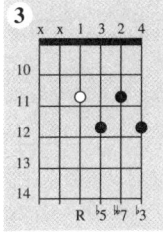

dim7(°7)
1, ♭3, ♭5, ♭♭7

D

Maj
1, 3, 5

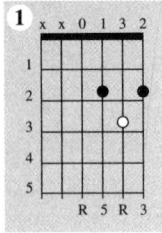 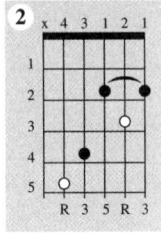 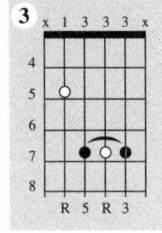 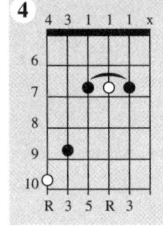 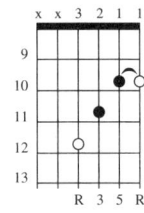 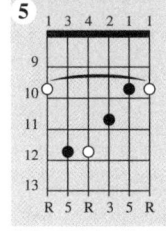

sus2
1, 2, 5

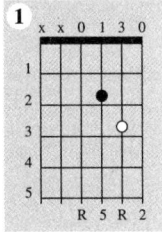 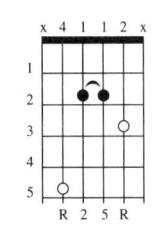 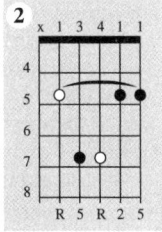 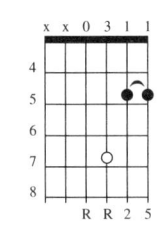 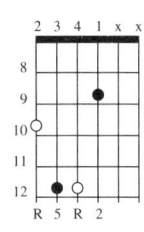 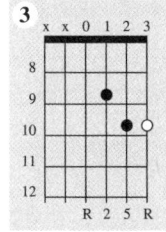

sus4
1, 4, 5

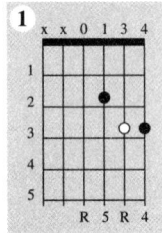 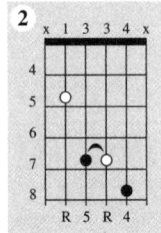 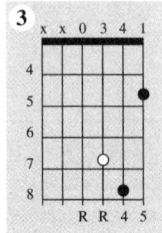 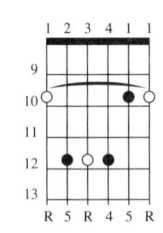 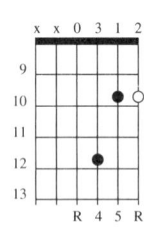 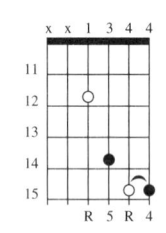

no 3rd
1, 5

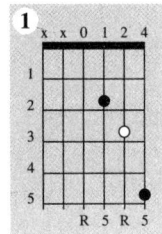 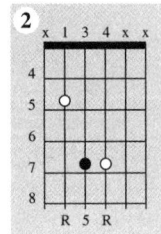 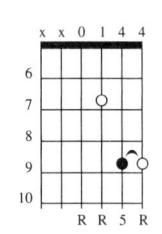 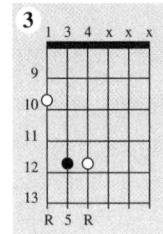 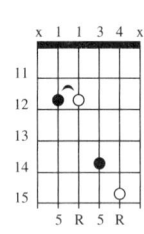

6
1, 3, 5, 6

 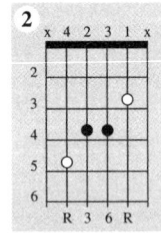 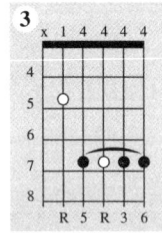 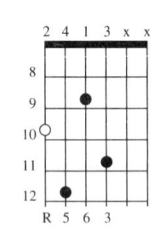 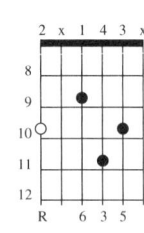 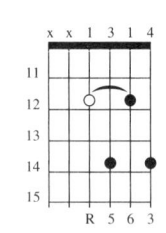

Maj7
1, 3, 5, 7

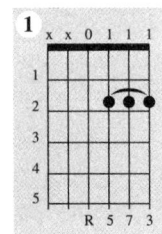 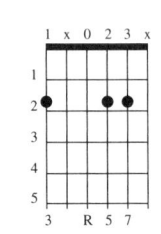 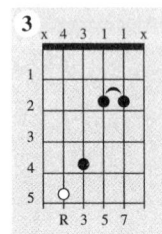 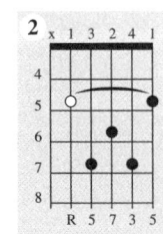 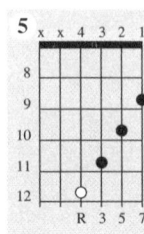 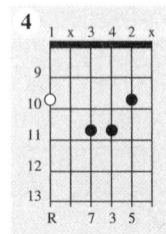

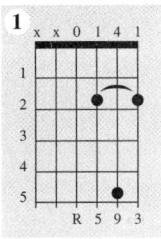 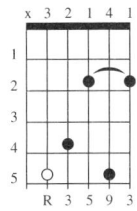 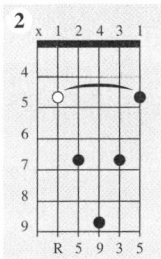 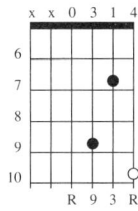 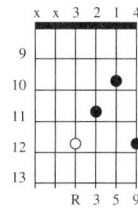 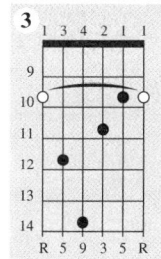

add9
1, 3, 5, 9

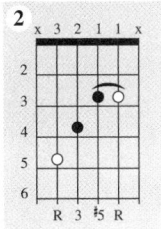 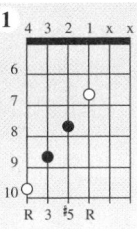 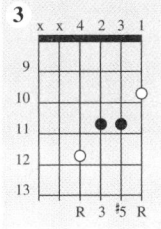

Augmented (aug)
1, 3, ♯5

D

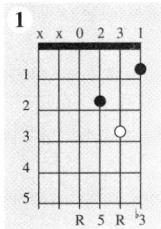 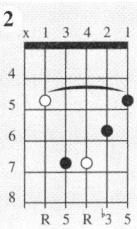 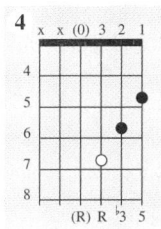 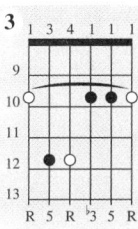 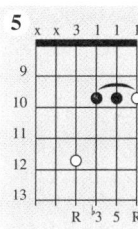 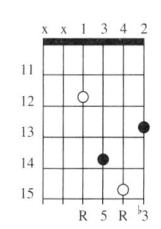

min
1, ♭3, 5

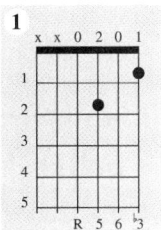 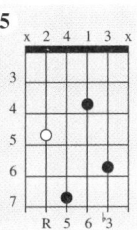 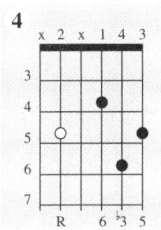 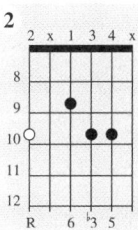 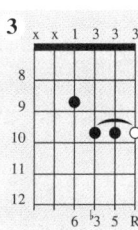 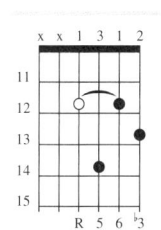

min6
1, ♭3, 5, 6

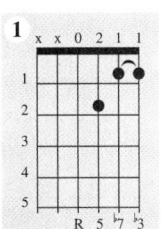 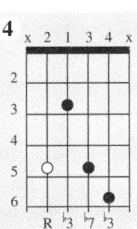 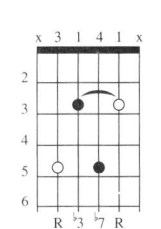 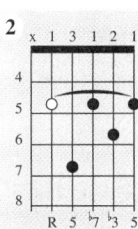  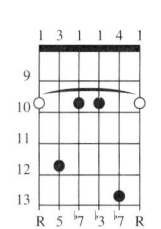

min7
1, ♭3, 5, ♭7

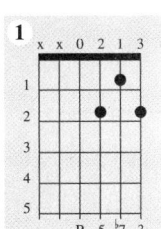 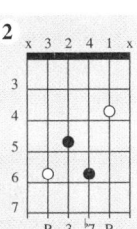 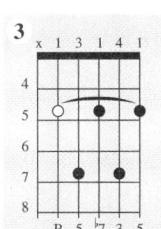 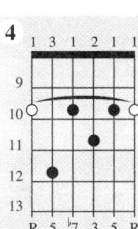 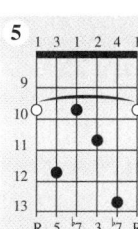 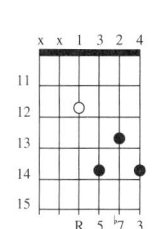

7
1, 3, 5, ♭7

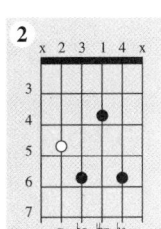 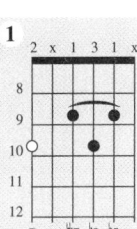 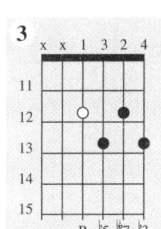

dim7(°7)
1, ♭3, ♭5, ♭♭7

Maj
1, 3, 5

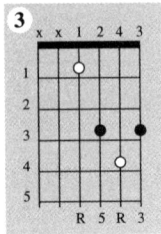 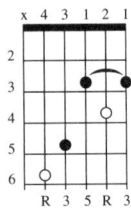 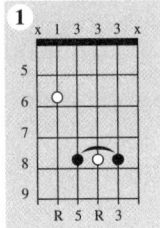 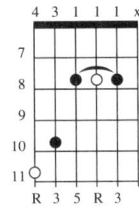 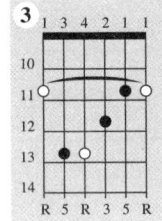 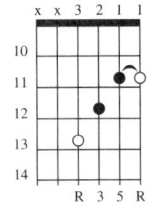

sus2
1, 2, 5

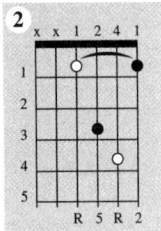 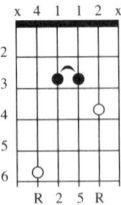 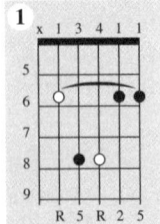 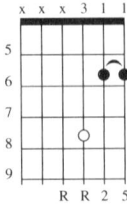 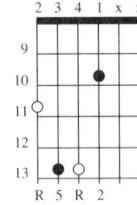

sus4
1, 4, 5

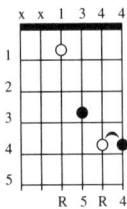 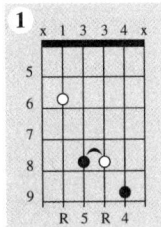 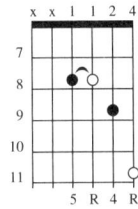 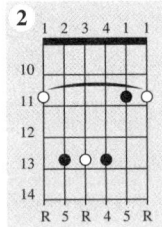

no 3rd
1, 5

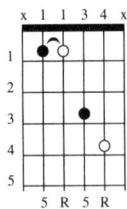 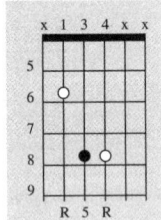 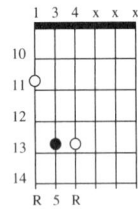

6
1, 3, 5, 6

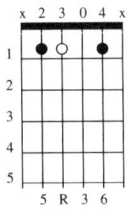 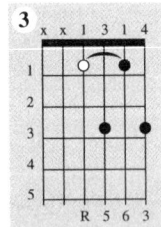 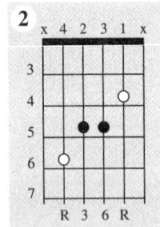 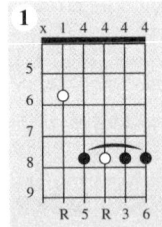 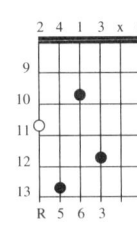 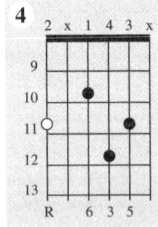

Maj7
1, 3, 5, 7

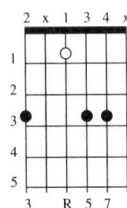 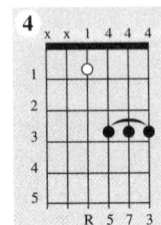 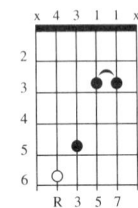   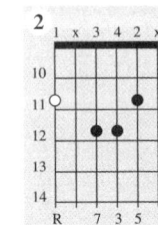

E♭
D♯

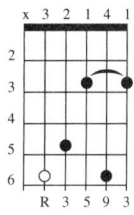 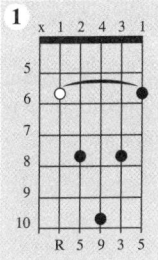 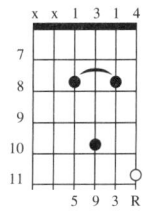 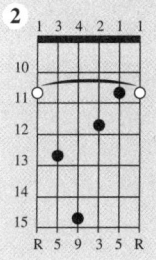 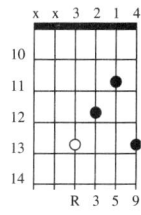

add9
1, 3, 5, 9

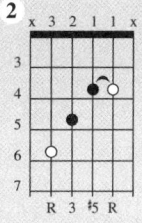 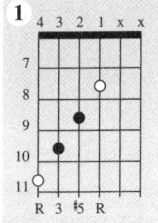 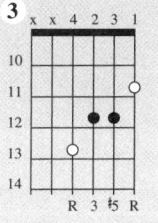

Augmented (aug)
1, 3, ♯5

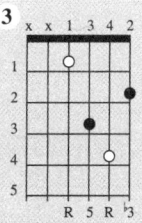 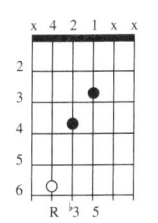 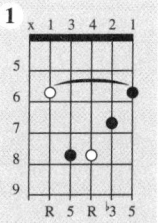 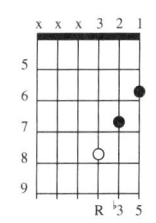 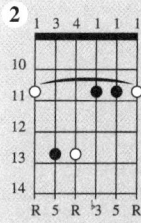 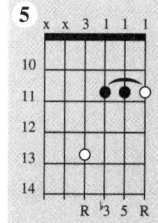

min
1, ♭3, 5

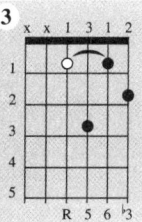 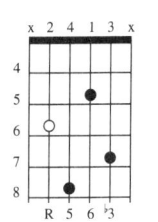 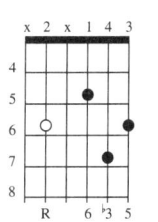 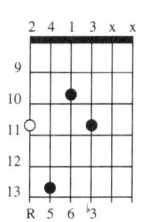 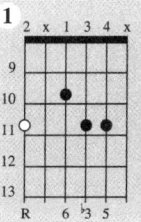 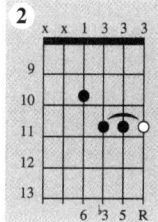

min6
1, ♭3, 5, 6

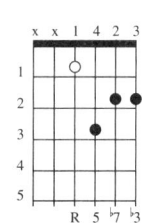 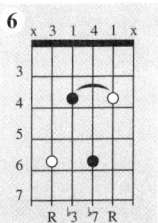 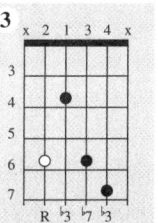 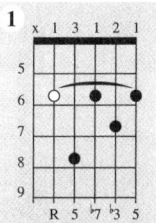 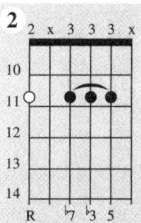 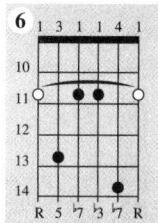

min7
1, ♭3, 5, ♭7

E♭
D♯

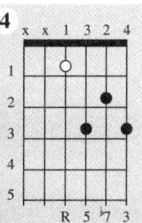 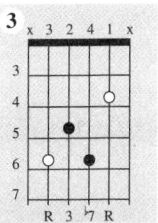 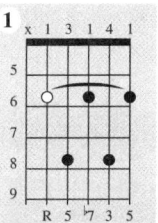 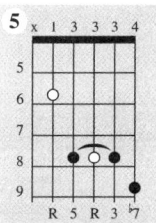 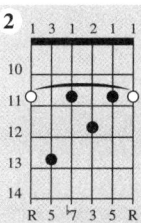 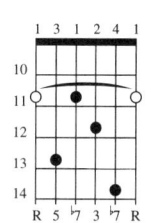

7
1, 3, 5, ♭7

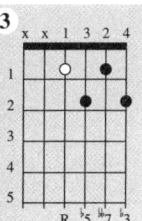 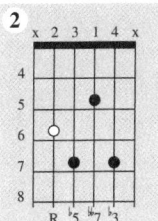 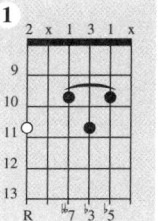

dim7(°7)
1, ♭3, ♭5, ♭♭7

E

Maj
1, 3, 5

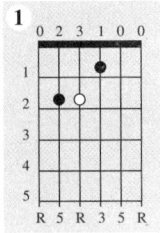 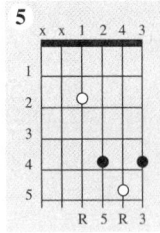 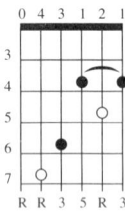 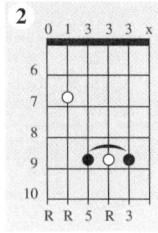 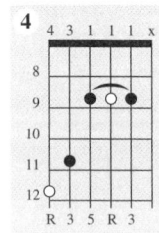 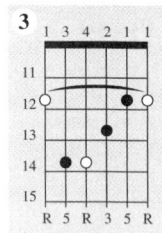

sus2
1, 2, 5

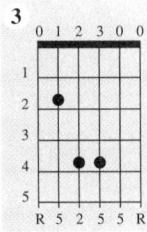 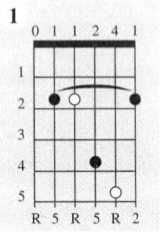 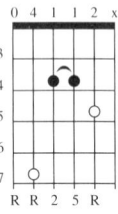 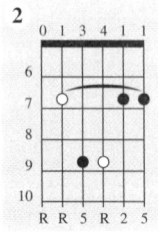 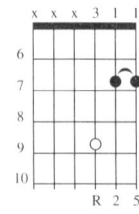 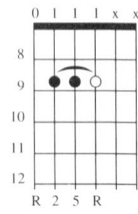

sus4
1, 4, 5

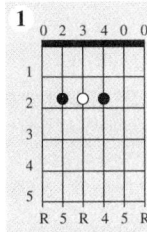 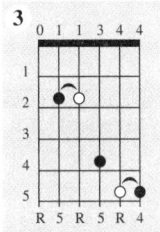 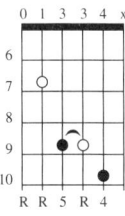 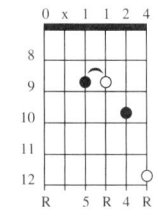 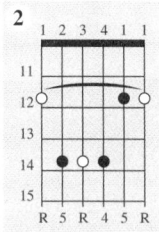

no 3rd
1, 5

 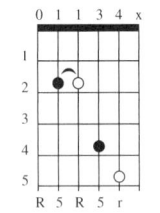 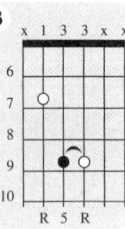 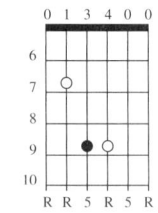 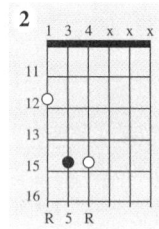

6
1, 3, 5, 6

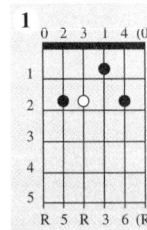 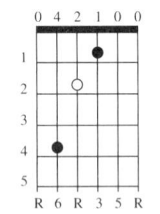  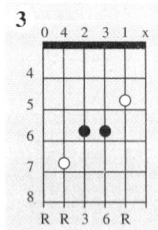 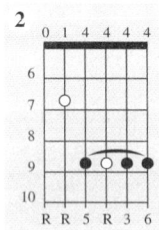 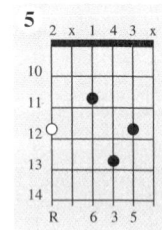

Maj7
1, 3, 5, 7

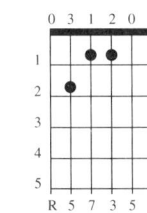 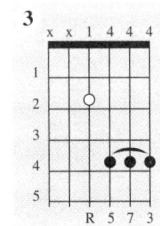  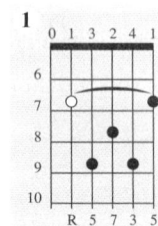 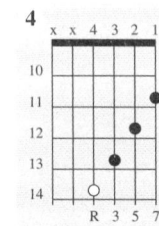 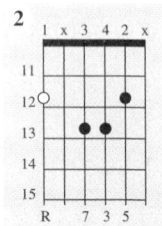

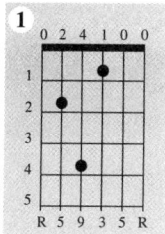 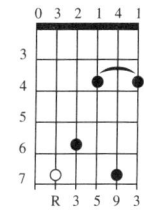 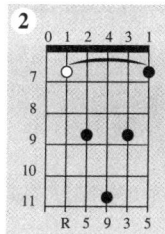 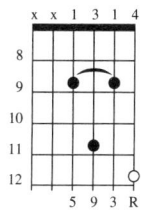 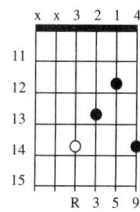 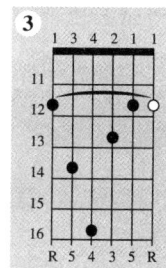

add9
1, 3, 5, 9

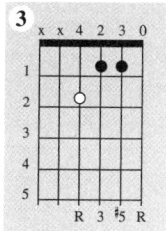 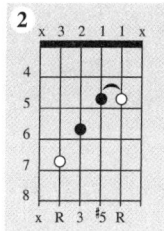 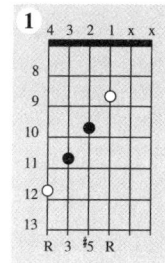

Augmented (aug)
1, 3, ♯5

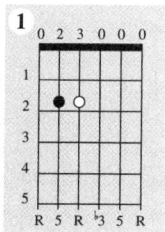 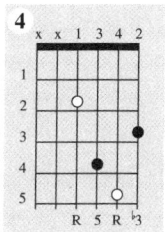 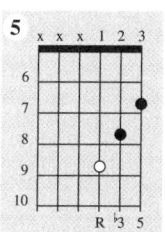 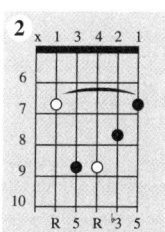 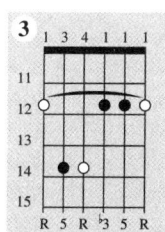 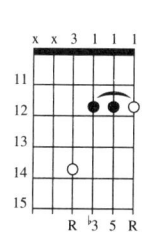

min
1, ♭3, 5

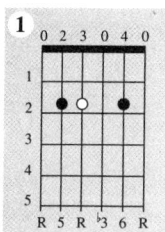 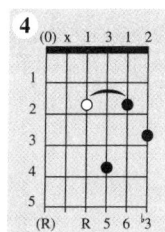 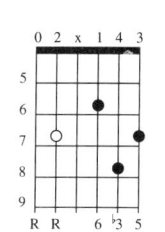 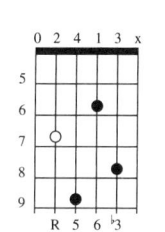 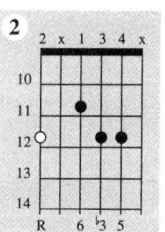 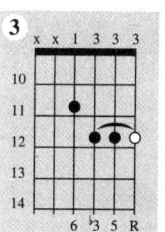

min6
1, ♭3, 5, 6

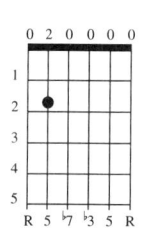 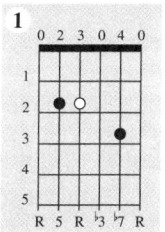 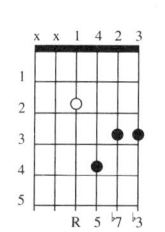 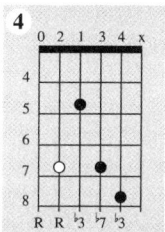 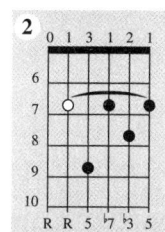 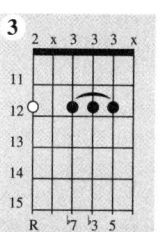

min7
1, ♭3, 5, ♭7

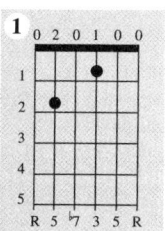 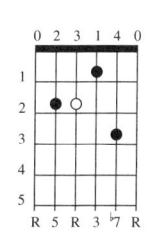 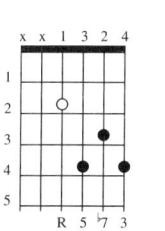 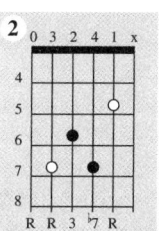 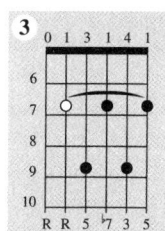 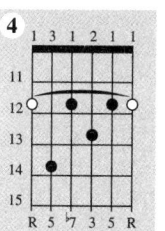

7
1, 3, 5, ♭7

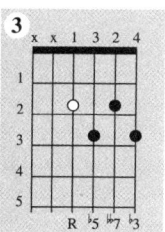 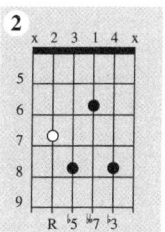 

dim7(°7)
1, ♭3, ♭5, ♭♭7

Maj
1, 3, 5

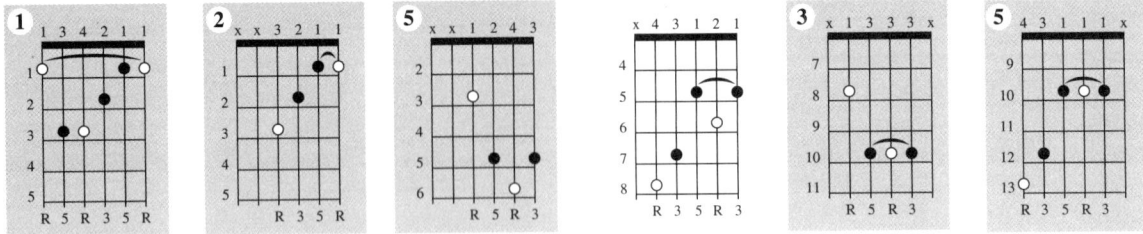

sus2
1, 2, 5

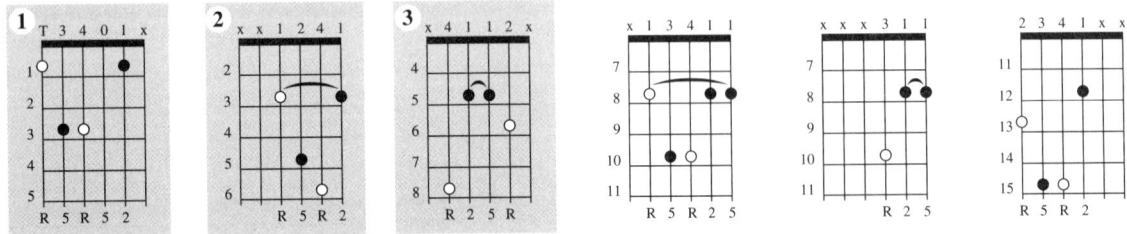

sus4
1, 4, 5

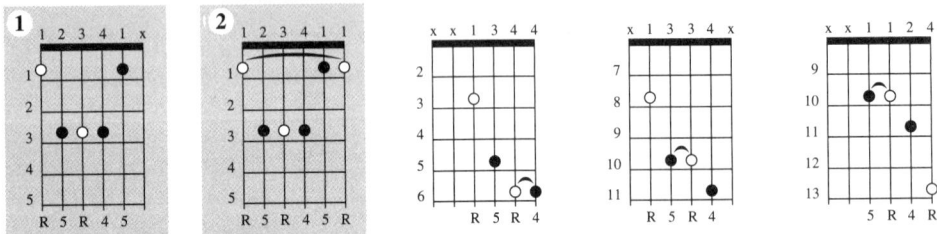

no 3rd
1, 5

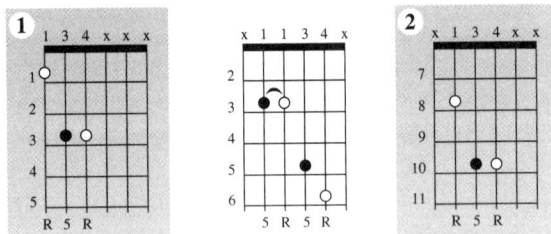

6
1, 3, 5, 6

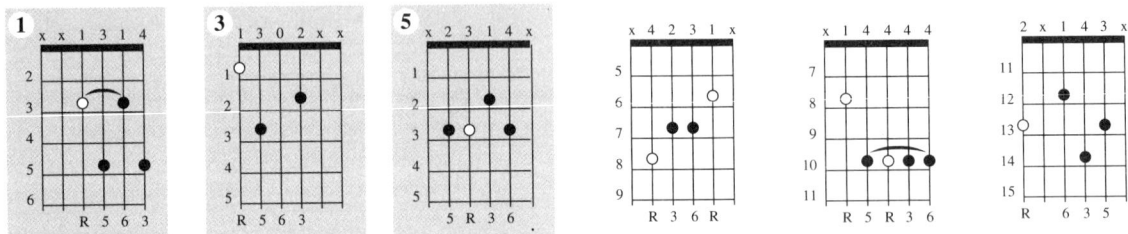

Maj7
1, 3, 5, 7

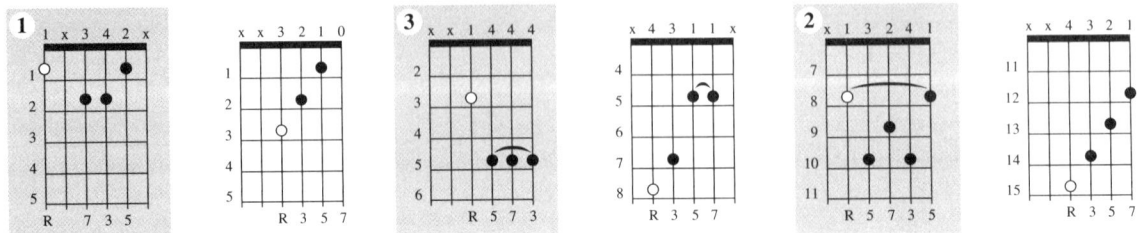

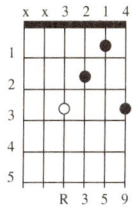 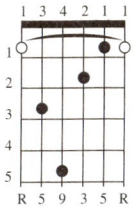 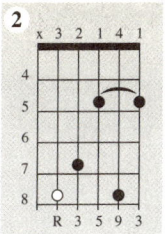 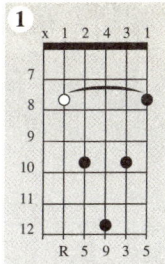 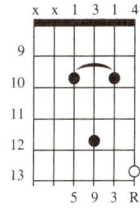

add9
1, 3, 5, 9

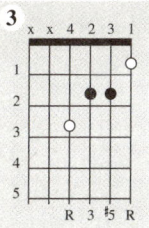 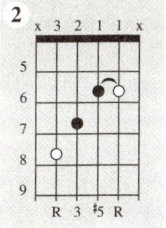 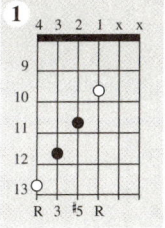

Augmented (aug)
1, 3, ♯5

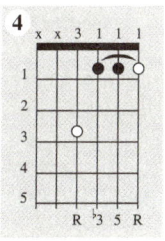 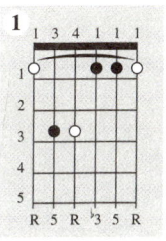 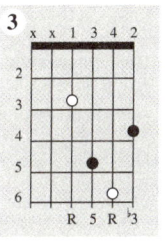 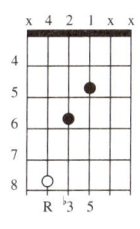 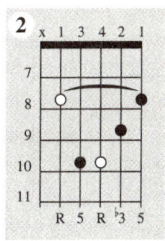 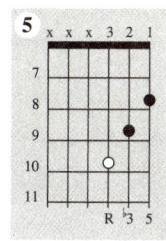

min
1, ♭3, 5

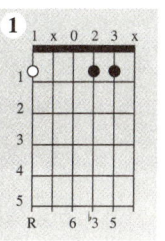 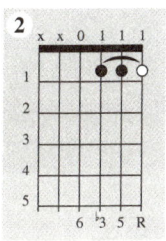 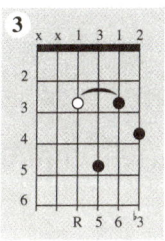 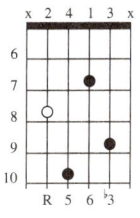 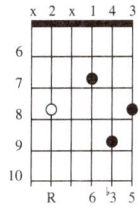 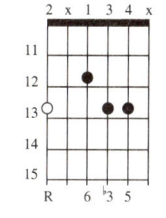

min6
1, ♭3, 5, 6

F

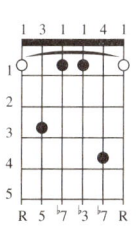 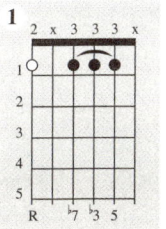 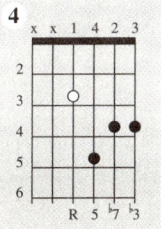 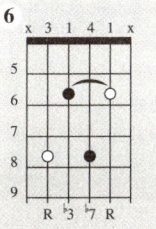 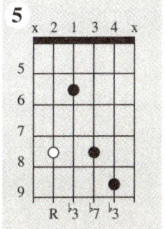 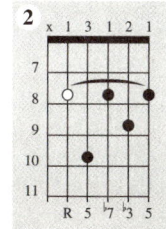

min7
1, ♭3, 5, ♭7

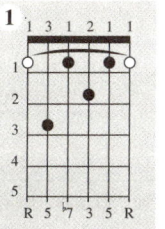 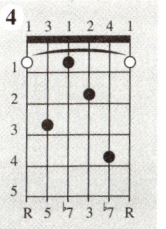 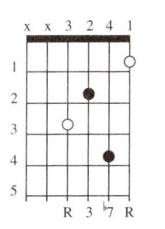 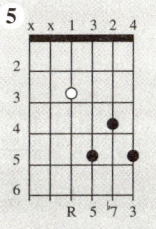 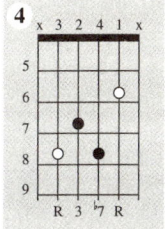 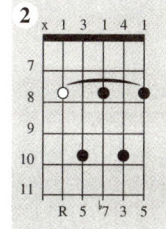

7
1, 3, 5, ♭7

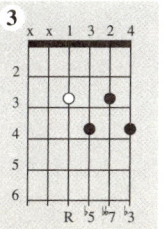 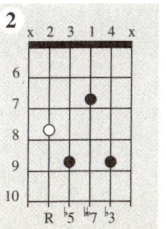 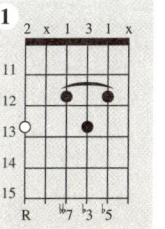

dim7 (°7)
1, ♭3, ♭5, ♭♭7

Maj
1, 3, 5

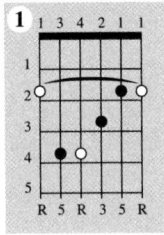 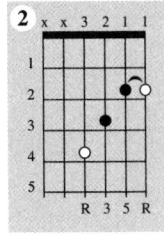 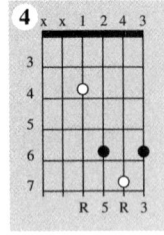 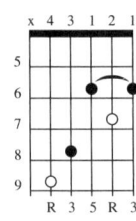 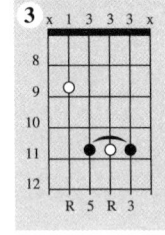 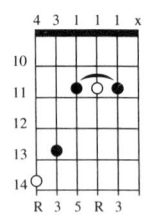

sus2
1, 2, 5

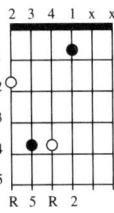 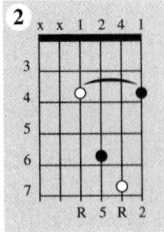 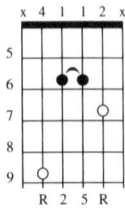 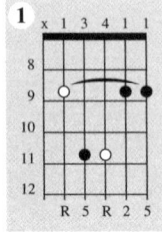 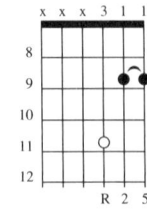

sus4
1, 4, 5

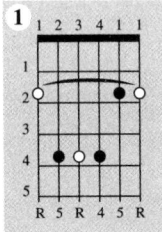 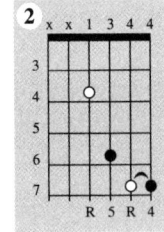 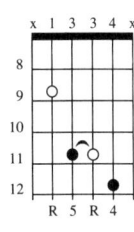 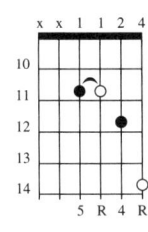

no 3rd
1, 5

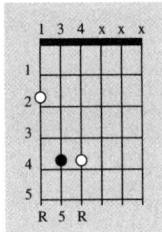 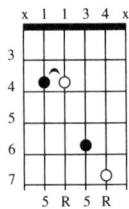 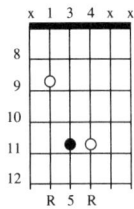

6
1, 3, 5, 6

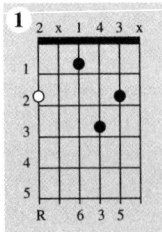 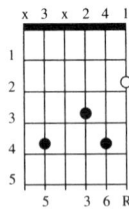 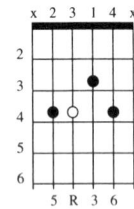 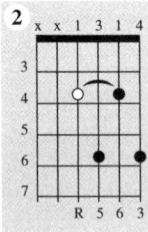 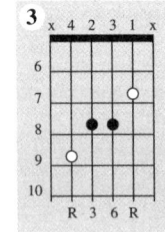 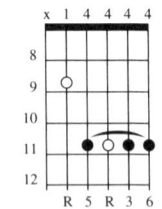

Maj7
1, 3, 5, 7

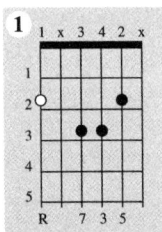 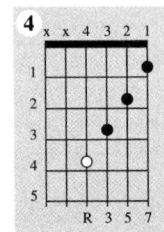 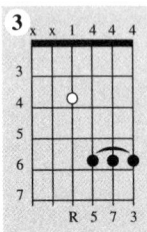 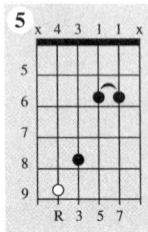 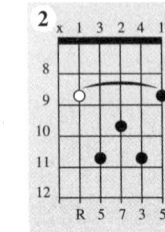 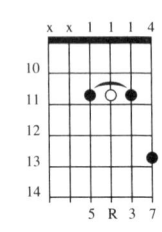

G♭
F♯

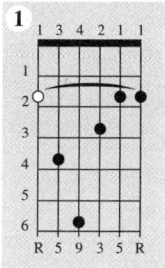 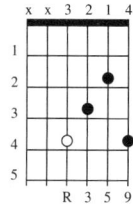 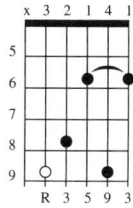 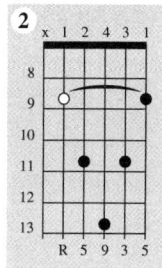 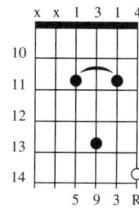

add9
1, 3, 5, 9

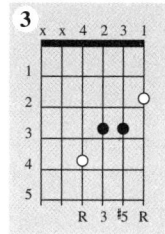 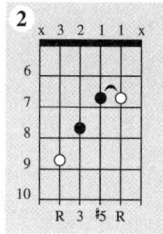 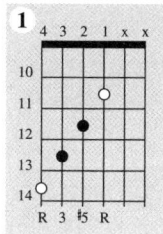

Augmented (aug)
1, 3, #5

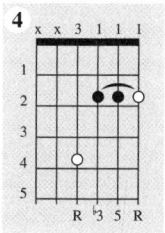 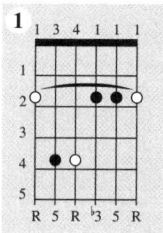 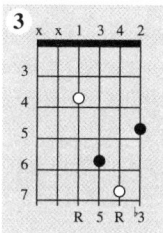 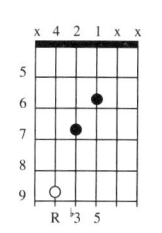 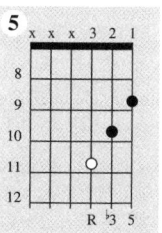 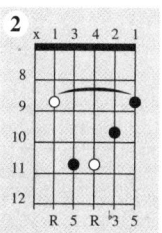

min
1, ♭3, 5

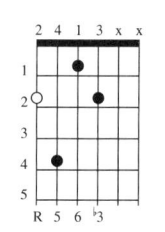 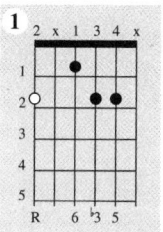 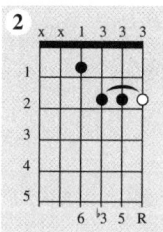 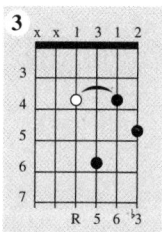 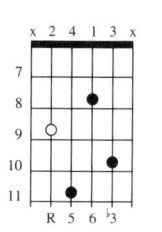 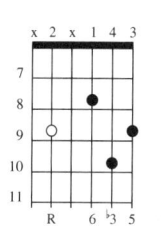

min6
1, ♭3, 5, 6

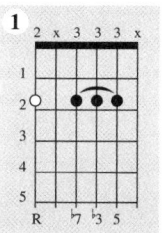 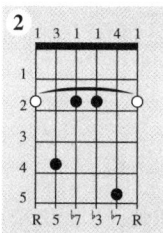 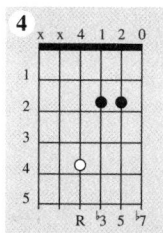 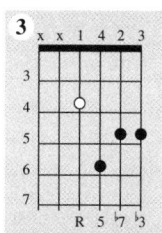 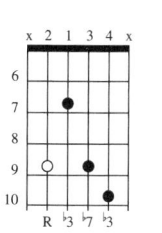 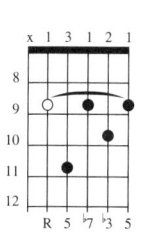

min7
1, ♭3, 5, ♭7

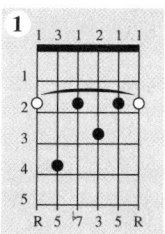 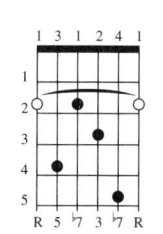 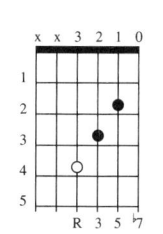 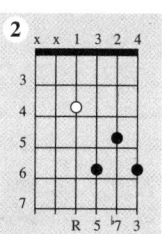 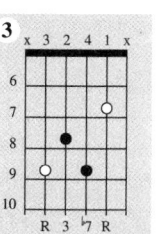 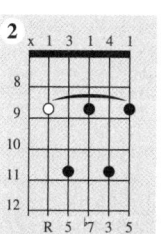

7
1, 3, 5, ♭7

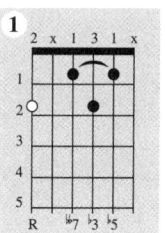 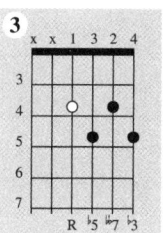 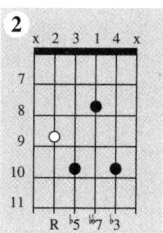

dim7(°7)
1, ♭3, ♭5, ♭♭7

G♭
F#

G

Maj
1, 3, 5

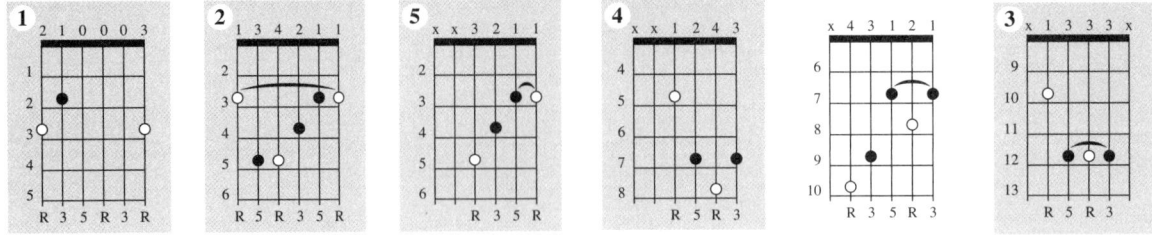

sus2
1, 2, 5

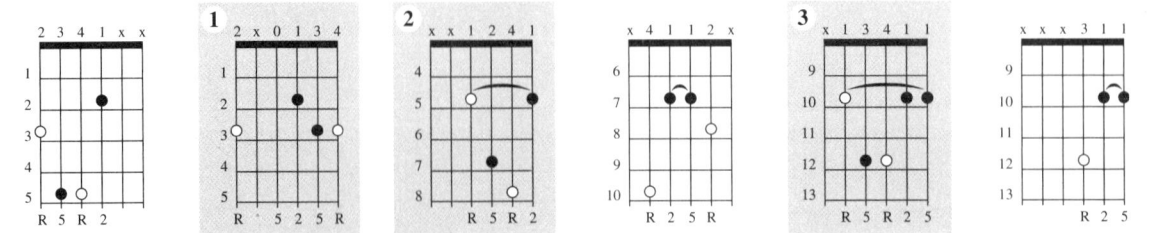

sus4
1, 4, 5

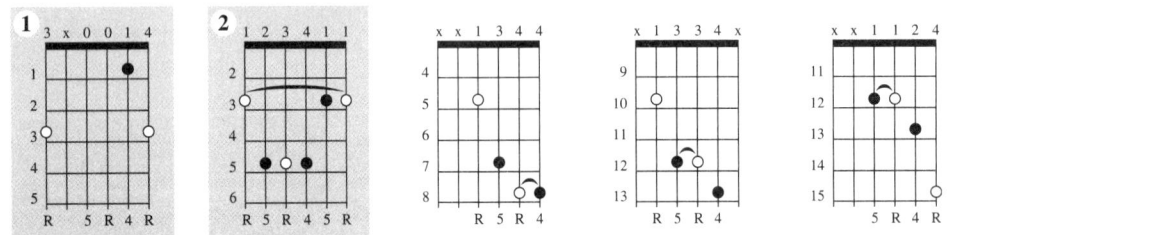

no 3rd
1, 5

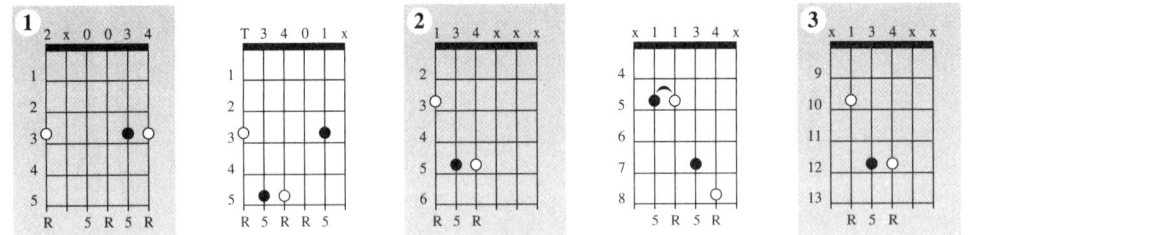

6
1, 3, 5, 6

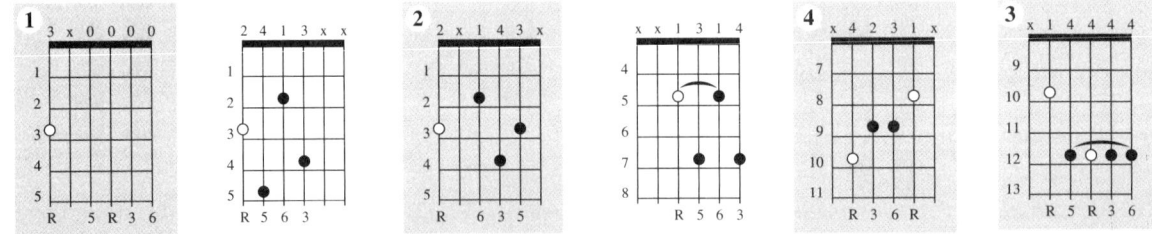

Maj7
1, 3, 5, 7

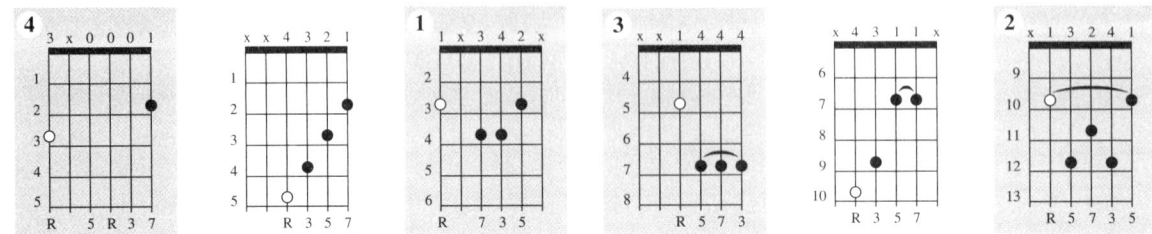

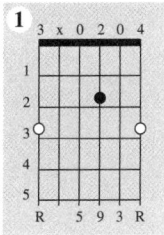 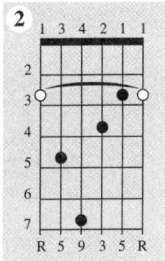 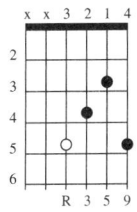 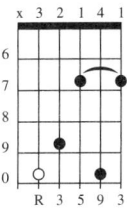 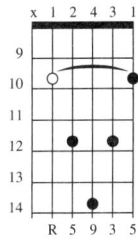 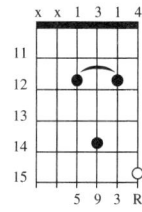

add9
1, 3, 5, 9

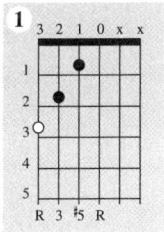 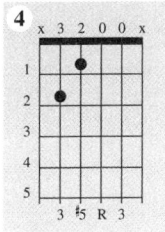 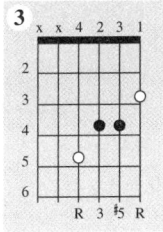 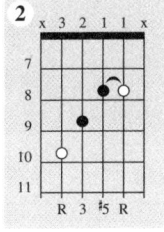

Augmented (aug)
1, 3, ♯5

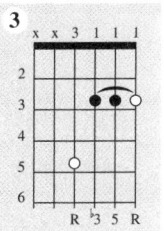 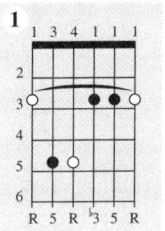 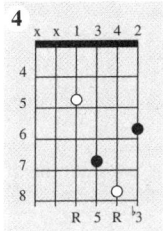 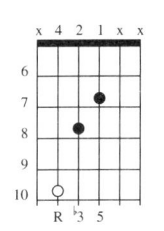 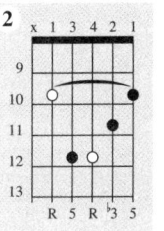 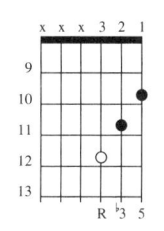

min
1, ♭3, 5

G

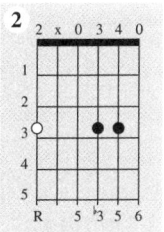 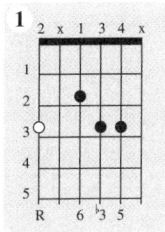 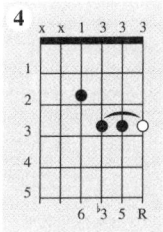 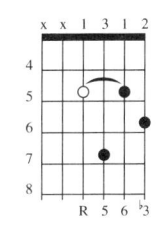 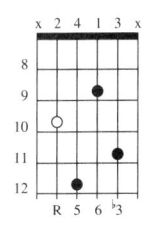 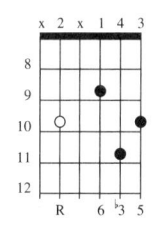

min6
1, ♭3, 5, 6

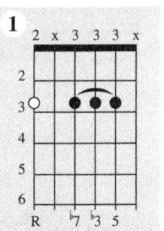 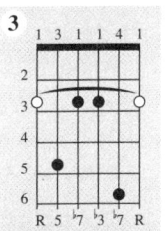 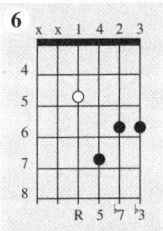 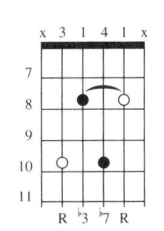 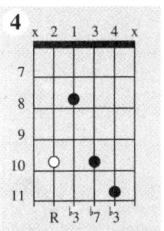 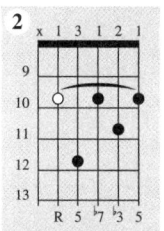

min7
1, ♭3, 5, ♭7

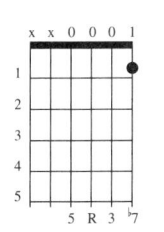 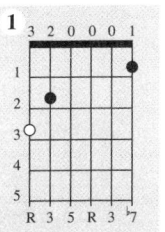 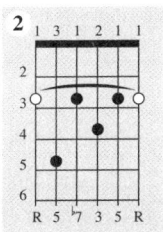 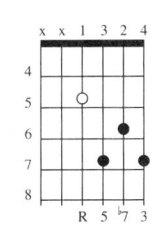 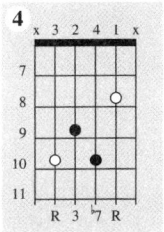 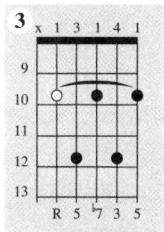

7
1, 3, 5, ♭7

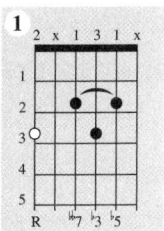 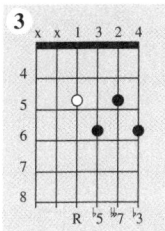 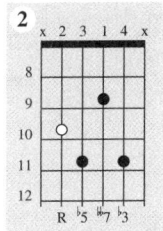

dim7(°7)
1, ♭3, ♭5, ♭♭7

Guitar Fretboard Chart

Frets 1–12

STRINGS

6th	5th	4th	3rd	2nd	1st
E	A	D	G	B	E

FRETS

STRINGS

FRETS	6th	5th	4th	3rd	2nd	1st
← Open →	E	A	D	G	B	E
← 1st Fret →	F	A#/B♭	D#/E♭	G#/A♭	C	F
← 2nd Fret →	F#/G♭	B	E	A	C#/D♭	F#/G♭
← 3rd Fret →	G	C	F	A#/B♭	D	G
← 4th Fret →	G#/A♭	C#/D♭	F#/G♭	B	D#/E♭	G#/A♭
← 5th Fret →	A	D	G	C	E	A
← 6th Fret →	A#/B♭	D#/E♭	G#/A♭	C#/D♭	F	A#/B♭
← 7th Fret →	B	E	A	D	F#/G♭	B
← 8th Fret →	C	F	A#/B♭	D#/E♭	G	C
← 9th Fret →	C#/D♭	F#/G♭	B	E	G#/A♭	C#/D♭
← 10th Fret →	D	G	C	F	A	D
← 11th Fret →	D#/E♭	G#/A♭	C#/D♭	F#/G♭	A#/B♭	D#/E♭
← 12th Fret →	E	A	D	G	B	E

Fretboard diagram (STRINGS 6th 5th 4th 3rd 2nd 1st — E A D G B E):

Fret	6th	5th	4th	3rd	2nd	1st
1st Fret	F	A#/B♭	D#/E♭	G#/A♭	C	F
2nd Fret	F#/G♭	B	E	A	C#/D♭	F#/G♭
3rd Fret	G	C	F	A#/B♭	D	G
4th Fret	G#/A♭	C#/D♭	F#/G♭	B	D#/E♭	G#/A♭
5th Fret	A	D	G	C	E	A
6th Fret	A#/B♭	D#/E♭	G#/A♭	C#/D♭	F	A#/B♭
7th Fret	B	E	A	D	F#/G♭	B
8th Fret	C	F	A#/B♭	D#/E♭	G	C
9th Fret	C#/D♭	F#/G♭	B	E	G#/A♭	C#/D♭
10th Fret	D	G	C	F	A	D
11th Fret	D#/E♭	G#/A♭	C#/D♭	F#/G♭	A#/B♭	D#/E♭
12th Fret	E	A	D	G	B	E

Conclusion

Congratulations! You've made it to the end of *The Total Beginning Guitarist*. You've learned a ton: chords, strum patterns, melodies, standard music notation, scale and chord theory, how to improvise basic solos, and a lot more. You are well on your way to becoming a great guitarist, but don't stop here. Listen to and play as much rock, blues, and jazz music as you can. Each of these genres has something unique to offer in terms of technique and style and will help you become a well-rounded player.

Learn about other types of music as well. For instance, we touched on fingerstyle playing in this book, but there is a whole world of great fingerstyle music and instructional materials available.

Play with as many people as you can. Seek out musicians who are more advanced than you—jamming with them can help you learn more and progress faster than if you were just locked away in your room practicing.

And finally, continue your studies. Find a teacher you admire, and also continue to learn from great instructional books and CDs, like the ones listed below.

Good luck, and enjoy!

Other Books from Alfred and the National Guitar Workshop:

Rock Guitar Method: Complete (Howard/Halbig)
Book & MP3CD (34346)

Blues Guitar Method: Complete (Hamburger/Smith/Riker)
Book & MP3CD (34349)

Jazz Guitar Method: Complete (Fisher)
Book & MP3CD (34352)

Fingerstyle Guitar Method: Complete (Manzi/Gunod/Eckels)
Book & MP3CD (36612)

Acoustic Blues Guitar Method: Complete (Manzi)
Book & MP3CD (36422)

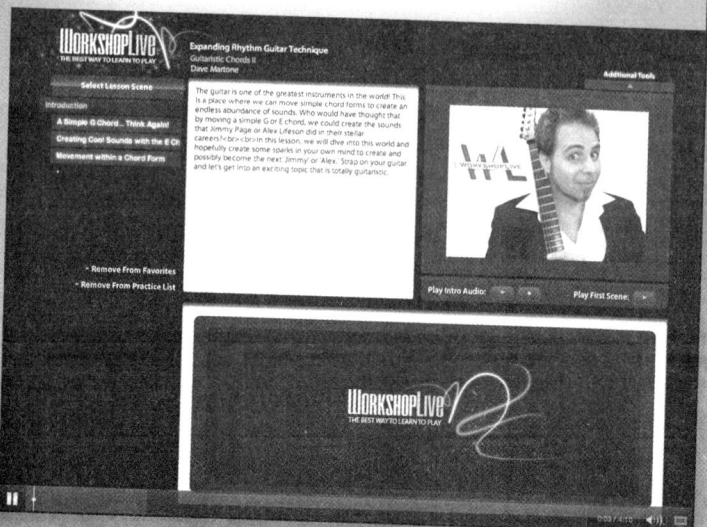